ENGLISH FAIRY·TALES

ENGLISH FAIRY·TALES

RETOLD·BY·FLORA·ANNIE·STEEL

ILLUSTRATED·BY
ARTHUR·RACKHAM

ABARIS · BOOKS

CONTENTS

The Wise Men of Gotham 7

Jack the Giant-Killer 17

The Three Little Pigs 41

Mr. and Mrs. Vinegar 49

Tattercoats 59

The Three Sillies 67

How Jack Went Out to Seek His Fortune 75

Dick Whittington and His Cat 81

Catskin 95

The Story of the Three Bears 103

The True History of Sir Thomas Thumb 111

Jack and the Beanstalk 121

The Fish and the Ring 137

The Bogey-Beast 145

The Two Sisters 153

The Golden Snuff-Box 163

List of Illustrations 175

THE WISE MEN OF GOTHAM

THE WISE MEN
OF GOTHAM

Of Buying of Sheep

There were two men of Gotham, and one of them was going to market to Nottingham to buy sheep, and the other came from the market, and they both met together upon Nottingham bridge.

"Where are you going?" said the one who came from Nottingham.

"Marry," said he that was going to Nottingham, "I am going to buy sheep."

"Buy sheep?" said the other; "and which way will you bring them home?

"Marry," said the other, "I will bring them over this bridge."

"By Robin Hood," said he that came from Nottingham, "but thou shalt not."

"By Maid Marion," said he that was going thither, "but I will."

"You will not," said the one.

"I will."

Then they beat their staves against the ground, one against the other, as if there had been a hundred sheep between them.

"Hold in," said one; "beware lest my sheep leap over the bridge."

"I care not," said the other; "they shall not come this way."

"But they shall," said the other.

Then the other said, "If that thou make much to do, I will put my fingers in thy mouth."

"Will you?" said the other.

Now, as they were at their contention, another man of Gotham came from the market with a sack of meal upon a horse, and seeing and hearing his neighbours at strife about sheep, though there were none between them, said:

"Ah, fools! will you ever learn wisdom? Help me, and lay my sack upon my shoulders."

They did so, and he went to the side of the bridge, unloosened the mouth of the sack, and shook all his meal out into the river.

"Now, neighbours," he said, "how much meal is there in my sack?"

"Marry," said they, "there is none at all."

"Now, by my faith," said he, "even as much wit as is in your two heads to stir up strife about a thing you have not."

Which was the wisest of these three persons, judge yourself.

Of Hedging a Cuckoo

Once upon a time the men of Gotham would have kept the Cuckoo so that she might sing all the year, and in the midst of their town they made a hedge round in compass and they got a Cuckoo, and put her into it, and said, "Sing there all through the year, or thou shalt have neither meat nor water." The Cuckoo, as soon as she perceived herself within the hedge, flew away. "A vengeance on her!" said they. "We did not make our hedge high enough."

Of Sending Cheeses

There was a man of Gotham who went to the market at Nottingham to sell cheese, and as he was going down the hill to Nottingham bridge, one of his cheeses fell out of his wallet and rolled down the hill. "Ah, gaffer," said the fellow, "can you run to market alone? I will send one after another after you." Then he laid down his wallet and took out the cheeses and rolled them down the hill. Some went into one bush, and some went into another.

"I charge you all to meet me near the market-place," cried he; and when the fellow came to the market to meet his cheeses, he stayed there till the market was nearly done. Then he went about to inquire of his friends and neighbours, and other men, if they did see his cheeses come to the market.

"Who should bring them?" said one of the market men.

"Marry, themselves," said the fellow; "they know the way well enough."

He said, "A vengeance on them all. I did fear, to see them run so fast, that they would run beyond the market. I am now fully persuaded that they must be now almost at York." Whereupon he forthwith hired a horse to ride to York, to seek his cheeses where they were not; but to this day no man can tell him of his cheeses.

Of Drowning Eels

When Good Friday came, the men of Gotham cast their heads together what to do with their white herrings, their red herrings, their sprats, and other salt fish. One consulted with the other, and agreed that such fish should be cast into their pond (which was in the middle of the town), that they might breed against the next year, and every man that had salt fish left cast them into the pool.

"I have many white herrings," said one.

"I have many sprats," said another.

"I have many red herrings," said the other.

"I have much salt fish. Let all go into the pond or pool, and we shall fare like lords next year."

At the beginning of next year following the men drew near the pond to have their fish, and there was nothing but a great eel. "Ah," said they all, "a mischief on this eel, for he has eaten up all our fish."

"What shall we do to him?" said one to the other.

"Kill him," said one.

"Chop him into pieces," said another.

"Not so," said another; "let us drown him."

"Be it so," said all. And they went to another pond, and cast the eel into the pond. "Lie there and shift for yourself, for no help thou shalt have from us"; and they left the eel to drown.

Of Sending Rent

Once on a time the men of Gotham had forgotten to pay their landlord. One said to the other, "Tomorrow is our pay-day, and what shall we find to send our money to our landlord?"

The one said, "This day I have caught a hare, and he shall carry it, for he is light of foot."

"Be it so," said all; "he shall have a letter and a purse to put our money in, and we shall direct him the right way." So when the letters were written and the money put in a purse, they tied it round the hare's neck, saying, "First you go to Lancaster, then thou must go to Loughborough, and Newarke is our landlord, and commend us to him, and there is his dues."

The hare, as soon as he was out of their hands, ran on along the country way. Some cried, "Thou must go to Lancaster first."

"Let the hare alone," said another; "he can tell a nearer way than the best of us all. Let him go."

Another said, "It is a subtle hare; let her alone; she will not keep the highway for fear of dogs."

Of Counting

On a certain time there were twelve men of Gotham who went fishing, and some went into the water and some on dry ground; and, as they were coming back, one of them said, "We have ventured much this day wading; I pray God that none of us that did come from home be drowned."

"Marry," said one, "let us see about that. Twelve of us came out." And every man did count eleven, and the twelfth man did never count himself.

"Alas!" said one to another, "one of us is drowned." They went back to the brook where they had been fishing, and looked up and down for him that was drowned, and made great lamentation. A courtier came riding by, and he did ask what they were seeking, and why they were so sorrowful. "Oh," said they, "this day we came to fish in this brook, and there were twelve of us, and one is drowned."

"Why," said the courtier, "count me how many of you there be"; and one counted eleven and did not count himself. "Well," said the courtier, "what will you give me if I find the twelfth man?"

"Sir," said they, "all the money we have."

"Give me the money," said the courtier; and he began with the first, and gave him a whack over the shoulders that he groaned, and said, "There is one, and he served all of them that they groaned; but when he came to the last he gave him a good blow, saying, "Here is the twelfth man."

"God bless you on your heart," said all the company; "you have found our neighbour."

JACK THE GIANT-KILLER

JACK THE GIANT-KILLER

I

When good King Arthur reigned with Guinevere his Queen, there lived, near the Land's End in Cornwall, a farmer who had one only son called Jack. Now Jack was brisk and ready; of such a lively wit that none nor nothing could worst him.

In those days, the Mount of St. Michael in Cornwall was the fastness of a hugeous giant whose name was Cormoran.

He was full eighteen feet in height, some three yards about his middle, of a grim fierce face, and he was the terror of all the country-side. He lived in a cave amidst the rocky Mount, and when he desired victuals he would wade across the tides to the mainland and furnish himself forth with all that came in his way. The poor folk and the rich folk alike ran out of their houses and hid themselves when they heard the swish-swash of his big feet in the water; for if he saw them, he would think nothing of broiling half-a-dozen or so of them for breakfast. As it was, he seized their cattle by the score, carrying off half-a-dozen fat oxen on his back at a time, and hanging sheep and pigs to his waistbelt like bunches of dip-candles. Now this had gone on for long years, and the poor folk of Cornwall were in despair, for none could put an end to the giant Cormoran.

It so happened that one market day Jack, then quite a young lad, found the town upside down over some new exploit of the giant's. Women were weeping, men were cursing, and the magistrates were sitting in Council over what was to be done. But none could suggest a plan. Then Jack, blithe and gay, went up to the magistrates, and with a fine courtesy—for he was ever polite—asked them what reward would be given to him who killed the giant Cormoran.

"The treasures of the Giant's Cave," quoth they.

"Every whit of it?" quoth Jack, who was never to be done.

"To the last farthing," quoth they.

"Then I will undertake the task," said Jack, and forthwith set about the business.

It was winter-time, and having got himself a horn, a pickaxe, and a shovel, he went over to the Mount in the dark evening, set to work, and before dawn he had dug a pit, no less than twenty-two feet deep and nigh as big across. This he covered with long thin sticks and straw, sprinkling a little loose mould over all to make it look like solid ground. So, just as dawn was breaking, he planted himself fair and square on the side of the pit that was farthest from the giant's cave, raised the horn to his lips, and with full blast sounded:

"Tantivy! Tantivy! Tantivy!"

just as he would have done had he been hunting a fox.

Of course this woke the giant, who rushed in a rage out of his cave, and seeing little Jack, fair and square blowing away at his horn, as calm and cool as may be, he became still more angry, and made for the disturber of his rest, bawling out, "I'll teach you to wake a giant, you little whipper-snapper. You shall pay dearly for your tantivys, I'll take you and broil you whole for break——"

He had only got as far as this when crash — he fell into the pit! So there was a break indeed; such an one that it caused the very foundations of the Mount to shake.

But Jack shook with laughter. "Ho, ho!" he cried, "how about breakfast now, Sir Giant? Will you have me broiled or baked? And will no diet serve you but poor little Jack? Faith! I've got you in Lob's pound now! You're in the stocks for bad behaviour, and I'll plague you as I like. Would I had rotten eggs; but this will do as well." And with that he up with his pickaxe and dealt the giant Cormoran such a most weighty knock on the very crown of his head, that he killed him on the spot.

Whereupon Jack calmly filled up the pit with earth again and went to search the cave, where he found much treasure.

Now when the magistrates heard of Jack's great exploit, they proclaimed

20

The giant Cormoran was the terror of all the country-side.

that henceforth he should be known as——

JACK THE GIANT-KILLER

And they presented him with a sword and belt, on which these words were embroidered in gold:

> Here's the valiant Cornishman
> Who slew the giant Cormoran.

II

Of course the news of Jack's victory soon spread over all England, so that another giant named Blunderbore who lived to the north, hearing of it, vowed if ever he came across Jack he would be revenged upon him. Now this giant Blunderbore was lord of an enchanted castle that stood in the middle of a lonesome forest.

It so happened that Jack, about four months after he had killed Cormoran, had occasion to journey into Wales, and on the road he passed this forest. Weary with walking, and finding a pleasant fountain by the wayside, he lay down to rest and was soon fast asleep.

Now the giant Blunderbore, coming to the well for water, found Jack sleeping, and knew by the lines embroidered on his belt that here was the far-famed giant-killer. Rejoiced at his luck, the giant, without more ado, lifted Jack to his shoulder and began to carry him through the wood to the enchanted castle.

But the rustling of the boughs awakened Jack, who, finding himself already in the clutches of the giant, was terrified; nor was his alarm decreased by seeing the courtyard of the castle all strewn with men's bones.

"Yours will be with them ere long," said Blunderbore as he locked poor Jack into an immense chamber above the castle gateway. It had a high-pitched beamed roof, and one window that looked down the road. Here poor Jack

JACK THE GIANT KILLER

was to stay while Blunderbore went to fetch his brother-giant, who lived in the same wood, that he might share in the feast.

Now, after a time, Jack, watching through the window, saw the two giants tramping hastily down the road, eager for their dinner.

"Now," quoth Jack to himself, "my death or my deliverance is at hand." For he had thought out a plan. In one corner of the room he had seen two strong cords. These he took, and making a cunning noose at the end of each, he hung them out of the window, and, as the giants were unlocking the iron door of the gate, managed to slip them over their heads without their noticing it. Then, quick as thought, he tied the other ends to a beam, so that as the giants moved on the nooses tightened and throttled them until they grew black in the face. Seeing this, Jack slid down the ropes, and drawing his sword, slew them both.

So, taking the keys of the castle, he unlocked all the doors and set free three beauteous ladies who, tied by the hair of their heads, he found almost starved to death.

"Sweet ladies," quoth Jack, kneeling on one knee—for he was ever polite—"here are the keys of this enchanted castle. I have destroyed the giant Blunderbore and his brutish brother, and thus have restored to you your liberty. These keys should bring you all else you require."

So saying he proceeded on his journey to Wales.

III

He travelled as fast as he could; perhaps too fast, for, losing his way, he found himself benighted and far from any habitation. He wandered on always in hopes, until on entering a narrow valley he came on a very large, dreary-looking house standing alone. Being anxious for shelter he went up to the door and knocked. You may imagine his surprise and alarm when the

Taking the keys of the castle, Jack unlocked all the doors.

summons was answered by a giant with two heads. But though this monster's look was exceedingly fierce, his manners were quite polite; the truth being that he was a Welsh giant, and as such double-faced and smooth, given to gaining his malicious ends by a show of false friendship.

So he welcomed Jack heartily in a strong Welsh accent, and prepared a bedroom for him, where he was left with kind wishes for a good rest. Jack, however, was too tired to sleep well, and as he lay awake, he overheard his host muttering to himself in the next room. Having very keen ears he was able to make out these words, or something like them:

"Though here you lodge with me this night,
You shall not see the morning light.
My club shall dash your brains outright."

"Say'st thou so!" quoth Jack to himself starting up at once. "So that is your Welsh trick, is it? But I will be even with you." Then, leaving his bed, he laid a big billet of wood among the blankets, and taking one of these to keep himself warm, made himself snug in a corner of the room, pretending to snore, so as to make Mr. Giant think he was asleep.

And sure enough, after a little time, in came the monster on tiptoe as if treading on eggs, and carrying a big club. Then——

WHACK! WHACK! WHACK!

Jack could hear the bed being belaboured until the Giant, thinking every bone of his guest's skin must be broken, stole out of the room again; whereupon Jack went calmly to bed once more and slept soundly! Next morning the giant couldn't believe his eyes when he saw Jack coming down the stairs fresh and hearty.

"Odds splutter hur nails!" he cried, astonished. "Did she sleep well? Was there not nothing felt in the night?"

"Oh," replied Jack, laughing in his sleeve, "I think a rat did come and give me two or three flaps of his tail."

On this the giant was dumbfounded, and led Jack to breakfast, bringing him a bowl which held at least four gallons of hasty-pudding, and bidding

27

him, as a man of such mettle, eat the lot. Now Jack when travelling wore under his cloak a leathern bag to carry his things withal; so, quick as thought, he hitched this round in front with the opening just under his chin; thus, as he ate, he could slip the best part of the pudding into it without the giant's being any the wiser. So they sate down to breakfast, the giant gobbling down his own measure of hasty-pudding, while Jack made away with his.

"See," says crafty Jack when he had finished. "I'll show you a trick worth two of yours," and with that he up with a carving-knife and, ripping up the leathern bag, out fell all the hasty-pudding on the floor!

"Odds splutter hur nails!" cried the giant, not to be outdone. "Hur can do that hurself!" Whereupon he seized the carving-knife, and ripping open his own belly fell down dead.

Thus was Jack quit of the Welsh giant.

IV

Now it so happened that in those days, when gallant knights were always seeking adventures, King Arthur's only son, a very valiant Prince, begged of his father a large sum of money to enable him to journey to Wales, and there strive to set free a certain beautiful lady who was possessed by seven evil spirits. In vain the King denied him; so at last he gave way and the Prince set out with two horses, one of which he rode, the other laden with goldpieces. Now after some days' journey the Prince came to a market-town in Wales where there was a great commotion. On asking the reason for it he was told that, according to law, the corpse of a very generous man had been arrested on its way to the grave, because, in life, it had owed large sums to the money-lenders.

"That is a cruel law," said the young Prince. "Go, bury the dead in peace, and let the creditors come to my lodgings; I will pay the debts of the dead."

So the creditors came, but they were so numerous that by evening the Prince had but twopence left for himself, and could not go further on his journey.

Now it so happened that Jack the Giant-Killer on his way to Wales passed through the town, and, hearing of the Prince's plight, was so taken with his kindness and generosity that he determined to be the Prince's servant. So this was agreed upon, and next morning, after Jack had paid the reckoning with his last farthing, the two set out together. But as they were leaving the town, an old woman ran after the Prince and called out, "Justice! Justice! The dead man owed me twopence these seven years. Pay me as well as the others."

And the Prince, kind and generous, put his hand to his pocket and gave the old woman the twopence that was left to him. So now they had not a penny between them, and when the sun grew low the Prince said:

"Jack! Since we have no money, how are we to get a night's lodging?"

Then Jack replied, "We shall do well enough, Master; for within two or three miles of this place there lives a huge and monstrous giant with three heads, who can fight four hundred men in armour and make them fly from him like chaff before the wind."

"And what good will that be to us?" quoth the Prince. "He will for sure chop us up in a mouthful."

"Nay," said Jack, laughing. "Let me go and prepare the way for you. By all accounts this giant is a dolt. Mayhap I may manage better than that."

So the Prince remained where he was, and Jack pricked his steed at full speed till he came to the giant's castle, at the gate of which he knocked so loud that he made the neighbouring hills resound.

On this the giant roared from within in a voice like thunder:

"Who's there?"

Then said Jack as bold as brass, "None but your poor cousin Jack."

"Cousin Jack!" quoth the giant, astounded. "And what news with my poor cousin Jack?" For, see you, he was quite taken aback; so Jack made haste to reassure him.

"Dear coz, heavy news, God wot!"

"Heavy news," echoed the giant, half afraid. "God wot, no heavy news can come to me. Have I not three heads? Can I not fight five hundred men in armour? Can I not make them fly like chaff before the wind?"

"True," replied crafty Jack, "but I came to warn you because the great King Arthur's son with a thousand men in armour is on his way to kill you."

At this the giant began to shiver and to shake. "Ah! Cousin Jack! Kind cousin Jack! This is heavy news indeed," quoth he. "Tell me, what am I to do?"

"Hide yourself in the vault," says crafty Jack, "and I will lock and bolt and bar you in, and keep the key till the Prince has gone. So you will be safe."

Then the giant made haste and ran down into the vault, and Jack locked, and bolted, and barred him in. Then being thus secure, he went and fetched his master, and the two made themselves heartily merry over what the giant was to have had for supper, while the miserable monster shivered and shook with fright in the underground vault.

Well, after a good night's rest Jack woke his master in early morn, and having furnished him well with gold and silver from the giant's treasure, bade him ride three miles forward on his journey. So when Jack judged that the Prince was pretty well out of the smell of the giant, he took the key and let his prisoner out. He was half dead with cold and damp, but very grateful; and he begged Jack to let him know what he would be given as a reward for saving the giant's life and castle from destruction, and he should have it.

"You're very welcome," said Jack, who always had his eyes about him. "All I want is the old coat and cap, together with the rusty old sword and slippers which are at your bed-head."

When the giant heard this he sighed and shook his head. "You don't know what you are asking," quoth he. "They are the most precious things I possess, but as I have promised, you must have them. The coat will make you invisible, the cap will tell you all you want to know, the sword will cut asunder whatever you strike, and the slippers will take you wherever you want to go in the twinkling of an eye!"

So Jack, overjoyed, rode away with the coat and cap, the sword and the slippers, and soon overtook his master; and they rode on together until they reached the castle where the beautiful lady lived whom the Prince sought.

Now she was very beautiful, for all she was possessed of seven devils, and when she heard the Prince sought her as a suitor, she smiled and ordered a

The Giant Galligantua and the wicked old magician transform the
duke's daughter into a white hind.

splendid banquet to be prepared for his reception. And she sate on his right hand, and plied him with food and drink.

And when the repast was over she took out her own handkerchief and wiped his lips gently, and said, with a smile:

"I have a task for you, my lord! You must show me that kerchief to-morrow morning or lose your head."

And with that she put the handkerchief in her bosom and said, "Good-night!"

The Prince was in despair, but Jack said nothing till his master was in bed. Then he put on the old cap he had got from the giant, and lo! in a minute he knew all that he wanted to know. So, in the dead of the night, when the beautiful lady called on one of her familiar spirits to carry her to Lucifer himself, Jack was beforehand with her, and putting on his coat of darkness and his slippers of swiftness, was there as soon as she was. And when she gave the handkerchief to the Devil, bidding him keep it safe, and he put it away on a high shelf, Jack just up and nipped it away in a trice!

So the next morning, when the beauteous enchanted lady looked to see the Prince crestfallen, he just made a fine bow and presented her with the handkerchief.

At first she was terribly disappointed, but, as the day drew on, she ordered another and still more splendid repast to be got ready. And this time, when the repast was over, she kissed the Prince full on the lips and said:

"I have a task for you, my lover. Show me to-morrow morning the last lips I kiss to-night or you lose your head."

Then the Prince, who by this time was head over ears in love, said tenderly, "if you will kiss none but mine, I will."

Now the beauteous lady, for all she was possessed by seven devils, could not but see that the Prince was a very handsome young man; so she blushed a little, and said:

"That is neither here nor there: you must show me them, or death is your portion."

So the Prince went to his bed, sorrowful as before; but Jack put on the cap of knowledge and knew in a moment all he wanted to know.

Thus when, in the dead of the night, the beauteous lady called on her familiar spirit to take her to Lucifer himself, Jack in his coat of darkness and his shoes of swiftness was there before her.

"Thou hast betrayed me once," said the beauteous lady to Lucifer, frowning, "by letting go my handkerchief. Now will I give thee something none can steal, and so best the Prince, King's son though he be."

With that she kissed the loathly demon full on the lips, and left him. Whereupon Jack with one blow of the rusty sword of strength cut off Lucifer's head, and, hiding it under his coat of darkness, brought it back to his master.

Thus next morning when the beauteous lady, with malice in her beautiful eyes, asked the Prince to show her the lips she had last kissed, he pulled out the demon's head by the horns. On that the seven devils, which possessed the poor lady, gave seven dreadful shrieks and left her. Thus the enchantment being broken, she appeared in all her perfect beauty and goodness.

So she and the Prince were married the very next morning. After which they journeyed back to the court of King Arthur, where Jack the Giant-Killer, for his many exploits, was made one of the Knights of the Round Table.

V

This, however, did not satisfy our hero, who was soon on the road again searching for giants. Now he had not gone far when he came upon one, seated on a huge block of timber near the entrance to a dark cave. He was a most terrific giant. His goggle eyes were as coals of fire, his countenance was grim and gruesome; his cheeks, like huge flitches of bacon, which resembled rods of iron wire, while the locks of hair that fell on his brawny shoulders showed like curled snakes or hissing adders. He held a knotted iron club, and breathed so heavily you could hear him a mile away. Nothing daunted by this fearsome sight, Jack alighted from his horse and, putting on his coat of darkness, went close up to the giant and said softly: "Hullo! is that you? It will not be long before I have you fast by your beard."

So saying he made a cut with the sword of strength at the giant's head, but, somehow, missing his aim, cut off the nose instead, clean as a whistle! My goodness! How the giant roared! It was like claps of thunder, and he began to lay about him with the knotted iron club, like one possessed. But Jack in his coat of darkness easily dodged the blows, and running in behind, drove the sword up to the hilt into the giant's back, so that he fell stone dead.

Jack then cut off the head and sent it to King Arthur by a waggoner whom he hired for the purpose. After which he began to search the giant's cave to find his treasure. He passed through many windings and turnings until he came to a huge hall paved and roofed with freestone. At the upper end of this was an immense fireplace where hung an iron cauldron, the like of which, for size, Jack had never seen before. It was boiling and gave out a savoury steam; while beside it, on the right hand, stood a big massive table set out with huge platters and mugs. Here it was that the giants used to dine. Going a little further he came upon a sort of window barred with iron, and looking within beheld a vast number of miserable captives.

"Alas! Alack!" they cried on seeing him. "Art come, young man, to join us in this dreadful prison?"

"That depends," quoth Jack; "but first tell me wherefore you are thus held imprisoned?"

"Through no fault," they cried at once. "We are captives of the cruel giants and are kept here and well nourished until such time as the monsters desire a feast. Then they choose the fattest and sup off them."

On hearing this Jack straightway unlocked the door of the prison and set the poor fellows free. Then, searching the giants' coffers, he divided the gold and silver equally amongst the captives as some redress for their sufferings, and taking them to a neighbouring castle gave them a right good feast.

VI

Now as they were all making merry over their deliverance, and praising Jack's prowess, a messenger arrived to say that one Thunderdell, a huge giant with two heads, having heard of the death of his kinsman, was on his way from the northern dales to be revenged, and was already within a mile or two of the castle, the country folk with their flocks and herds flying before him like chaff before the wind.

Now the castle with its gardens stood on a small island that was surrounded by a moat twenty feet wide and thirty feet deep, having very steep sides. And this moat was spanned by a drawbridge. This, without a moment's delay, Jack ordered should be sawn on both sides at the middle, so as to only leave one plank uncut over which he in his invisible coat of darkness passed swiftly to meet his enemy, bearing in his hand the wonderful sword of strength.

Now though the giant could not, of course, see Jack, he could smell him, for giants have keen noses. Therefore Thunderdell cried out in a voice like his name:

"Fee, fi, fo, fum!
I smell the blood of an Englishman.
Be he alive, or be he dead,
I'll grind his bones to make my bread!"

"Is that so?" quoth Jack, cheerful as ever. "Then art thou a monstrous miller for sure!"

On this the giant, peering round everywhere for a glimpse of his foe, shouted out:

"Art thou, indeed, the villain who hath killed so many of my kinsmen? Then, indeed, will I tear thee to pieces with my teeth, suck thy blood, and grind thy bones to powder."

"Thou'lt have to catch me first," quoth Jack, laughing, and throwing off his coat of darkness and putting on his slippers of swiftness, he began nimbly to lead the giant a pretty dance, he leaping and doubling light as a feather, the monster following heavily like a walking tower, so that the very foundation of the earth seemed to shake at every step. At this game the onlookers nearly split their sides with laughter, until Jack, judging there had been enough of it, made for the drawbridge, ran neatly over the single plank, and reaching the other side waited in teasing fashion for his adversary.

On came the giant at full speed, foaming at the mouth with rage, and flourishing his club. But when he came to the middle of the bridge his great weight, of course, broke the plank, and there he was fallen headlong into the moat, rolling and wallowing like a whale, plunging from place to place, yet unable to get out and be revenged.

The spectators greeted his efforts with roars of laughter, and Jack himself was at first too overcome with merriment to do more than scoff. At last, however, he went for a rope, cast it over the giant's two heads, so, with the help of a team of horses, drew them shorewards, where two blows from the sword of strength settled the matter.

VII

After some time spent in mirth and pastimes, Jack began once more to grow restless, and taking leave of his companions set out for fresh adventures.

He travelled far and fast, through woods, and vales, and hills, till at last he came, late at night, on a lonesome house set at the foot of a high mountain.

Knocking at the door, it was opened by an old man whose head was white as snow.

"Father," said Jack, ever courteous, "can you lodge a benighted traveller?"

"Ay, that will I, and welcome to my poor cottage," replied the old man.

Whereupon Jack came in, and after supper they sate together chatting in friendly fashion. Then it was that the old man, seeing by Jack's belt that he was the famous Giant-Killer, spoke in this wise:

"My son! You are the great conqueror of evil monsters. Now close by there lives one well worthy of your prowess. On the top of yonder high hill is an enchanted castle kept by a giant named Galligantua, who, by the help of a wicked old magician, inveigles many beautiful ladies and valiant knights into the castle, where they are transformed into all sorts of birds and beasts, yea, even into fishes and insects. There they live pitiably in confinement; but most of all do I grieve for a duke's daughter whom they kidnapped in her father's garden, bringing her hither in a burning chariot drawn by fiery dragons. Her form is that of a white hind; and though many valiant knights have tried their utmost to break the spell and work her deliverance, none have succeeded; for, see you, at the entrance to the castle are two dreadful griffins who destroy every one who attempts to pass them by."

Now Jack bethought him of the coat of darkness which had served him so well before, and he put on the cap of knowledge, and in an instant he knew what had to be done. Then the very next morning, at dawn-time, Jack arose and put on his invisible coat and his slippers of swiftness. And in the twinkling of an eye there he was on the top of the mountain! And there were the two griffins guarding the castle gates—horrible creatures with forked tails and tongues. But they could not see him because of the coat of darkness, so he passed them by unharmed.

And hung to the doors of the gateway he found a golden trumpet on a silver chain, and beneath it was engraved in red lettering:

Whoever shall this trumpet blow
Will cause the giant's overthrow.
The black enchantment he will break,
And gladness out of sadness make.

No sooner had Jack read these words than he put the horn to his lips and blew a loud

"Tantivy!   Tantivy!   Tantivy!"

Now at the very first note the castle trembled to its vast foundations, and before he had finished the measure, both the giant and the magician were biting their thumbs and tearing their hair, knowing that their wickedness must now come to an end. But the giant showed fight and took up his club to defend himself; whereupon Jack, with one clean cut of the sword of strength, severed his head from his body, and would doubtless have done the same to the magician, but that the latter was a coward, and, calling up a whirlwind, was swept away by it into the air, nor has he ever been seen or heard of since. The enchantments being thus broken, all the valiant knights and beautiful ladies, who had been transformed into birds and beasts and fishes and reptiles and insects, returned to their proper shapes, including the duke's daughter, who, from being a white hind, showed as the most beauteous maiden upon whom the sun ever shone. Now, no sooner had this occurred than the whole castle vanished away in a cloud of smoke, and from that moment giants vanished also from the land.

So Jack, when he had presented the head of Galligantua to King Arthur, together with all the lords and ladies he had delivered from enchantment, found he had nothing more to do. As a reward for past services, however, King Arthur bestowed the hand of the duke's daughter upon honest Jack the Giant-Killer. So married they were, and the whole kingdom was filled with joy at their wedding. Furthermore, the King bestowed on Jack a noble castle with a magnificent estate belonging thereto, whereon he, his lady, and their children lived in great joy and content for the rest of their days.

THE THREE LITTLE PIGS

THE THREE LITTLE PIGS

Once upon a time there was an old sow who had three little pigs, and as she had not enough for them to eat, she said they had better go out into the world and seek their fortunes.

Now the eldest pig went first, and as he trotted along the road he met a man carrying a bundle of straw. So he said very politely:

"If you please, sir, could you give me that straw to build me a house?"

And the man, seeing what good manners the little pig had, gave him the straw, and the little pig set to work and built a beautiful house with it.

Now, when it was finished, a wolf happened to pass that way; and he saw the house, and *he smelt the pig inside.*

So he knocked at the door and said:

"Little pig! Little pig! Let me in! Let me in!"

But the little pig saw the wolf's big paws through the keyhole, so he answered back:

"No! No! No! by the hair of my chinny chin chin!"

Then the wolf showed his teeth and said:

"Then I'll huff and I'll puff and I'll blow your house in."

So he huffed and he puffed and he blew the house in. Then he ate up little piggy and went on his way.

Now, the next piggy, when he started, met a man carrying a bundle of furze, and, being very polite, he said to him:

"If you please, sir, could you give me that furze to build me a house?"

And the man, seeing what good manners the little pig had, gave him the furze, and the little pig set to work and built himself a beautiful house.

Now it so happened that when the house was finished the wolf passed that way; and he saw the house, and *he smelt the pig inside.*

So he knocked at the door and said:

"Little pig! Little pig! Let me in! Let me in!"

But the little pig peeped through the keyhole and saw the wolf's great ears, so he answered back:

No! No! No! by the hair of my chinny chin chin!"

Then the wolf showed his teeth and said:

"Then I'll huff and I'll puff and I'll blow your house in!"

So he huffed and he puffed and he blew the house in. Then he ate up little piggy and went on his way.

Now the third little piggy, when he started, met a man carrying a load of bricks, and, being very polite, he said:

"If you please, sir, could you give me those bricks to build me a house?"

And the man, seeing that he had been well brought up, gave him the bricks, and the little pig set to work and built himself a beautiful house.

And once again it happened that when it was finished the wolf chanced to come that way; and he saw the house, and *he smelt the pig inside.*

So he knocked at the door and said:

"Little pig! Little pig! Let me in! Let me in!"

But the little pig peeped through the keyhole and saw the wolf's great eyes, so he answered:

"No! No! No! by the hair of my chinny chin chin!"

"Then I'll huff and I'll puff and I'll blow your house in!" says the wolf, showing his teeth.

Well! he huffed and he puffed. He puffed and he huffed. And he huffed, huffed, and he puffed, puffed; but he could *not* blow the house down. At last he was so out of breath that he couldn't huff and he couldn't puff any more.

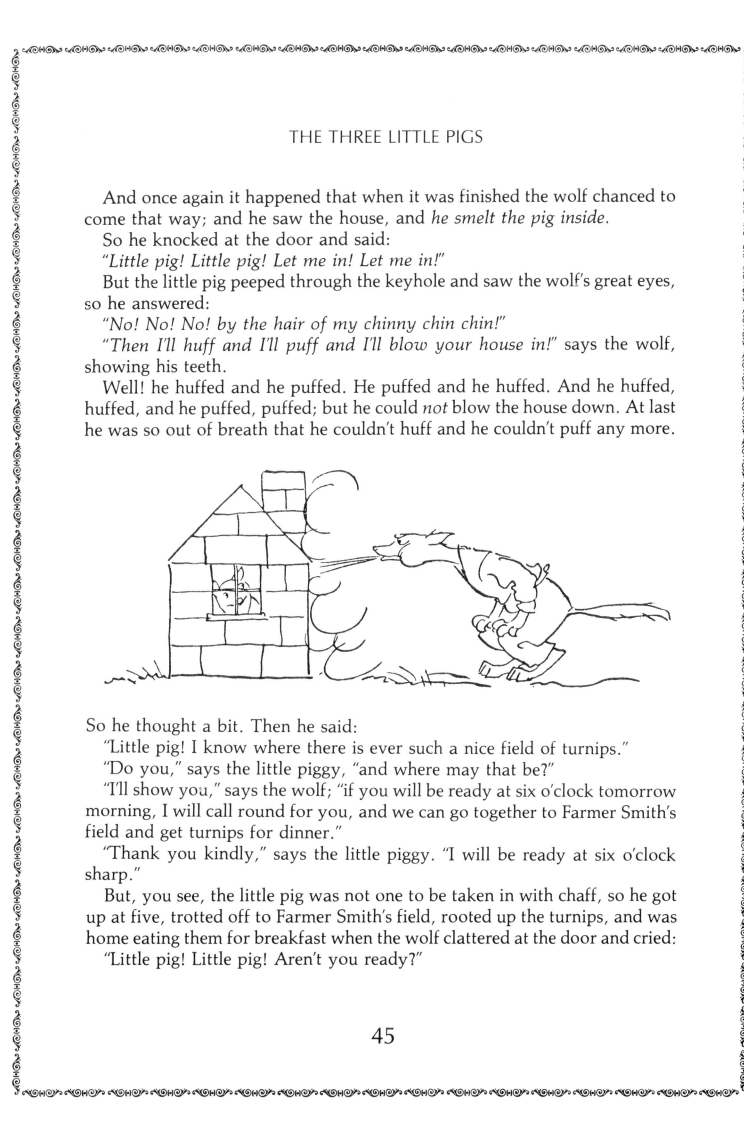

So he thought a bit. Then he said:

"Little pig! I know where there is ever such a nice field of turnips."

"Do you," says the little piggy, "and where may that be?"

"I'll show you," says the wolf; "if you will be ready at six o'clock tomorrow morning, I will call round for you, and we can go together to Farmer Smith's field and get turnips for dinner."

"Thank you kindly," says the little piggy. "I will be ready at six o'clock sharp."

But, you see, the little pig was not one to be taken in with chaff, so he got up at five, trotted off to Farmer Smith's field, rooted up the turnips, and was home eating them for breakfast when the wolf clattered at the door and cried:

"Little pig! Little pig! Aren't you ready?"

"Ready?" says the little piggy. "Why! what a sluggard you are! I've been to the field and come back again, and I'm having a nice potful of turnips for breakfast."

Then the wolf grew red with rage; but he was determined to eat little piggy, so he said, as if he didn't care:

"I'm glad you like them; but I know of something better than turnips."

"Indeed," says little piggy, "and what may that be?"

"A nice apple tree down in Merry gardens with the juiciest, sweetest apples on it! So if you will be ready at five o'clock tomorrow morning I will come round for you and we can get the apples together."

"Thank you kindly," says little piggy. "I will be sure and be ready at five o'clock sharp."

Now the next morning he bustled up ever so early, and it wasn't four o'clock when he started to get the apples; but, you see, the wolf had been taken in once and wasn't going to be taken in again, so he also started at four o'clock, and the little pig had but just got his basket half full of apples when he saw the wolf coming down the road licking his lips.

"Hullo!" says the wolf, "here already! You *are* an early bird! Are the apples nice?"

"Very nice," says little piggy; "I'll throw you down one to try."

And he threw it so far away, that when the wolf had gone to pick it up, the little pig was able to jump down with his basket and run home.

Well, the wolf was fair angry; but he went next day to the little piggy's house and called through the door, as mild as milk:

"Little pig! Little pig! You are so clever, I should like to give you a fairing; so if you will come with me to the fair this afternoon you shall have one."

"Thank you kindly," says little piggy. "What time shall we start?"

"At three o'clock sharp," says the wolf, "so be sure to be ready."

"I'll be ready before three," sniggered the little piggy. And he was! He started early in the morning and went to the fair, and rode in a swing, and enjoyed himself ever so much, and bought himself a butter-churn as a fairing, and trotted away towards home long before three o'clock. But just as he got to the top of the hill, what should he see but the wolf coming up it, all panting and red with rage!

Well, there was no place to hide in but the butter-churn; so he crept into it, and was just pulling down the cover when the churn started to roll down the hill—

Bumpety, bumpety, bump!

Of course piggy, inside, began to squeal, and when the wolf heard the noise, and saw the butter-churn rolling down on top of him—

Bumpety, bumpety, bump!

—he was so frightened that he turned tail and ran away. But he was still determined to get the little pig for his dinner; so he went next day to the house and told the little pig how sorry he was not to have been able to keep his promise of going to the fair, because of an awful, dreadful, terrible Thing that had rushed at him, making a fearsome noise.

"Dear me!" says the little piggy, "that must have been me! I hid inside the butter-churn when I saw you coming, and it started to roll! I am sorry I frightened you!"

But this was too much. The wolf danced about with rage and swore he would come down the chimney and eat up the little pig for supper. But while he was climbing on to the roof the little pig made up a blazing fire and put on a big pot full of water to boil. Then, just as the wolf was coming down the chimney, the little piggy off with the lid, and plump! in fell the wolf into the scalding water.

So the little piggy put on the cover again, boiled the wolf up, and ate *him* for supper.

MR. AND MRS. VINEGAR

MR. AND MRS. VINEGAR

Mr. and Mrs. Vinegar, a worthy couple, lived in a glass pickle-jar. The house, though small, was snug, and so light that each speck of dust on the furniture showed like a mole-hill; so while Mr. Vinegar tilled his garden with a pickle-fork and grew vegetables for pickling, Mrs. Vinegar, who was a sharp, bustling, tidy woman, swept, brushed, and dusted, brushed and dusted and swept to keep the house clean as a new pin. Now one day she lost her temper with a cobweb and swept so hard after it that bang! bang! the broom-handle went right through the glass, and crash! crash! clitter! clatter! there was the pickle-jar house about her ears all in splinters and bits.

She picked her way over these as best she might, and rushed into the garden.

"Oh, Vinegar, Vinegar!" she cried. "We are clean ruined and done for! Quit these vegetables! they won't be wanted! What is the use of pickles if you haven't a pickle-jar to put them in, and—I've broken ours—into little bits!" And with that she fell to crying bitterly.

But Mr. Vinegar was of different mettle; though a small man, he was a cheerful one, always looking at the best side of things, so he said, "Accidents will happen, lovey! But there are as good pickle-bottles in the shop as ever came out of it. All we need is money to buy another. So let us go out into the world and seek our fortunes."

"But what about the furniture?" sobbed Mrs. Vinegar.

"I will take the door of the house with me, lovey," quoth Mr. Vinegar stoutly. "Then no one will be able to open it, will they?"

Mrs. Vinegar did not quite see how this fact would mend matters, but, being a good wife, she held her peace. So off they trudged into the world to seek fortune, Mr. Vinegar bearing the door on his back like a snail carries its house.

Well, they walked all day long, but not a brass farthing did they make, and when night fell they found themselves in a dark, thick forest. Now Mrs.

Vinegar, for all she was a smart, strong woman, was tired to death, and filled with fear of wild beasts, so she began once more to cry bitterly; but Mr. Vinegar was cheerful as ever.

"Don't alarm yourself, lovey," he said. "I will climb into a tree, fix the door firmly in a fork, and you can sleep there as safe and comfortable as in your own bed."

So he climbed the tree, fixed the door, and Mrs. Vinegar lay down on it, and being dead tired was soon fast asleep. But her weight tilted the door sideways, so, after a time, Mr. Vinegar, being afraid she might slip off, sate down on the other side to balance her and keep watch.

Now in the very middle of the night, just as he was beginning to nod, what should happen but that a band of robbers should meet beneath that very tree in order to divide their spoils. Mr. Vinegar could hear every word said quite distinctly, and began to tremble like an aspen as he listened to the terrible deeds the thieves had done to gain their ends.

"Don't shake so!" murmured Mrs. Vinegar, half asleep. "You'll have me off the bed."

"I'm not shaking, lovey," whispered back Mr. Vinegar in a quaking voice. "It is only the wind in the trees."

But for all his cheerfulness he was not really *very* brave *inside*, so he went on trembling and shaking, and shaking and trembling, till, just as the robbers were beginning to parcel out the money, he actually shook the door right out of the tree-fork, and down it came—with Mrs. Vinegar still asleep upon it— right on top of the robbers' heads!

As you may imagine, they thought the sky had fallen, and made off as fast as their legs would carry them, leaving their booty behind them. But Mr. Vinegar, who had saved himself from the fall by clinging to a branch, was far too frightened to go down in the dark to see what had happened. So up in the tree he sate like a big bird until dawn came.

Then Mrs. Vinegar woke, rubbed her eyes, yawned, and said, "Where am I?"

"On the ground, lovey," answered Mr. Vinegar, scrambling down."

And when they lifted up the door, what do you think they found?

One robber squashed flat as a pancake, and forty golden guineas all scattered about!

My goodness! How Mr. and Mrs. Vinegar jumped for joy!

"Now, Vinegar!" said his wife when they had gathered up all the gold

Mr. and Mrs. Vinegar at home.

pieces, "I will tell you what we must do. You must go to the next market-town and buy a cow; for, see you, money makes the mare to go, truly; but it also goes itself. Now a cow won't run away, but will give us milk and butter, which we can sell. So we shall live in comfort for the rest of our days."

"What a head you have, lovey!" said Mr. Vinegar admiringly, and started off on his errand.

"Mind you make a good bargain," bawled his wife after him.

"I always do," bawled back Mr. Vinegar. "I made a good bargain when I married such a clever wife, and I made a better one when I shook her down from the tree. I am the happiest man alive!"

So he trudged on, laughing and jingling the forty gold pieces in his pocket.

Now the first thing he saw in the market was an old red cow.

"I am in luck to-day," he thought; "that is the very beast for me. I shall be the happiest of men if I get that cow." So he went up to the owner, jingling the gold in his pocket.

"What will you take for the cow?" he asked.

And the owner of the cow, seeing he was a simpleton, said, "What you've got in your pocket."

"Done!" said Mr. Vinegar, handed over the forty guineas, and led off the cow, marching her up and down the market, much against her will, to show off his bargain.

Now, as he drove it about, proud as Punch, he noticed a man who was playing the bagpipes. He was followed about by a crowd of children who danced to the music, and a perfect shower of pennies fell into his cap every time he held it out.

"Ho, ho!" thought Mr. Vinegar. "That is an easier way of earning a livelihood than by driving about a beast of a cow! Then the feeding, and the milking, and the churning! Ah, I should be the happiest man alive if I had those bagpipes!"

So he went up to the musician and said, "What will you take for your bagpipes?"

"Well," replied the musician, seeing he was a simpleton, "it is a beautiful instrument, and I make so much money by it, that I cannot take anything less than that red cow."

"Done!" cried Mr. Vinegar in a hurry, lest the man should repent of his offer.

So the musician walked off with the red cow, and Mr. Vinegar tried to play the bagpipes. But, alas and alack! though he blew till he almost burst, not a sound could he make at first, and when he did at last, it was such a terrific squeal and screech that all the children ran away frightened, and the people stopped their ears.

But he went on and on, trying to play a tune, and never earning anything, save hootings and peltings, until his fingers were almost frozen with the cold, when of course the noise he made on the bagpipes was worse than ever.

Then he noticed a man who had on a pair of warm gloves, and he said to himself, "Music is impossible when one's fingers are frozen. I believe I should be the happiest man alive if I had those gloves."

So he went up to the owner and said, "You seem, sir, to have a very good pair of gloves." And the man replied, "Truly, sir, my hands are as warm as toast this bitter November day."

That quite decided Mr. Vinegar, and he asked at once what the owner would take for them; and the owner, seeing he was a simpleton, said, "As your hands seem frozen, sir, I will, as a favour, let you have them for your bagpipes."

"Done!" cried Mr. Vinegar, delighted, and made the exchange.

Then he set off to find his wife, quite pleased with himself. "Warm hands, warm heart!" he thought. "I'm the happiest man alive!"

But as he trudged he grew very, very tired, and at last began to limp. Then he saw a man coming along the road with a stout stick.

"I should be the happiest man alive if I had that stick," he thought. "What is the use of warm hands if your feet ache!" So he said to the man with the stick, "What will you take for your stick?" and the man, seeing he was a simpleton, replied:

"Well, I don't want to part with my stick, but as you are so pressing I'll oblige you, as a friend, for those warm gloves you are wearing."

"Done for you!" cried Mr. Vinegar delightedly; and trudged off with the stick, chuckling to himself over his good bargain.

But as he went along a magpie fluttered out of the hedge and sate on a branch in front of him, and chuckled and laughed as magpies do. "What are you laughing at?" asked Mr. Vinegar.

"At you, forsooth!" chuckled the magpie, fluttering just a little further. "At *you*, Mr. Vinegar, you foolish man—you simpleton—you blockhead! You bought a cow for forty guineas when she wasn't worth ten, you exchanged

And that is the story of Mr. and Mrs. Vinegar.

her for bagpipes you couldn't play—you changed the bagpipes for a pair of gloves, and the pair of gloves for a miserable stick. Ho, ho! Ha, ha! So you've nothing to show for your forty guineas save a stick you might have cut in any hedge. Ah, you fool! you simpleton! you blockhead!"

And the magpie chuckled, and chuckled, and chuckled in such guffaws, fluttering from branch to branch as Mr. Vinegar trudged along, that at last he flew into a violent rage and flung his stick at the bird. And the stick stuck in a tree out of his reach; so he had to go back to his wife without anything at all.

But he was glad the stick had stuck in a tree, for Mrs. Vinegar's hands were quite hard enough.

When it was all over Mr. Vinegar said cheerfully, "You are too violent, lovey. You broke the pickle-jar, and now you've nearly broken every bone in my body. I think we had better turn over a new leaf and begin afresh. I shall take service as a gardener, and you can go as a housemaid, until we have enough money to buy a new pickle-jar. There are as good ones in a shop as ever came out of it."

And that is the story of Mr. and Mrs. Vinegar.

TATTERCOATS

TATTERCOATS

In a great Palace by the sea there once dwelt a very rich old lord, who had neither wife nor children living, only one little granddaughter, whose face he had never seen in all her life. He hated her bitterly, because at her birth his favourite daughter died; and when the old nurse brought him the baby he swore that it might live or die as it liked, but he would never look on its face as long as it lived.

So he turned his back, and sat by his window looking out over the sea, and weeping great tears for his lost daughter, till his white hair and beard grew down over his shoulders and twined round his chair and crept into the chinks of the floor, and his tears, dropping on to the window-ledge, wore a channel through the stone, and ran away in a little river to the great sea. Meanwhile, his granddaughter grew up with no one to care for her, or clothe her; only the old nurse, when no one was by, would sometimes give her a dish of scraps from the kitchen, or a torn petticoat from the rag-bag; while the other servants of the palace would drive her from the house with blows and mocking words, calling her "Tattercoats," and pointing to her bare feet and shoulders, till she ran away, crying, to hide among the bushes.

So she grew up, with little to eat or to wear, spending her days out of doors, her only companion a crippled gooseherd, who fed his flock of geese on the common. And this gooseherd was a queer, merry little chap, and when she was hungry, or cold, or tired, he would play to her so gaily on his little pipe, that she forgot all her troubles, and would fall to dancing with his flock of noisy geese for partners.

Now one day people told each other that the King was travelling through the land, and was to give a great ball to all the lords and ladies of the country in the town near by, and that the Prince, his only son, was to choose a wife from amongst the maidens in the company. In due time one of the royal invitations to the ball was brought to the Palace by the sea, and the servants carried it up to the old lord, who still sat by his window, wrapped in his long white hair and weeping into the little river that was fed by his tears.

But when he heard the King's command, he dried his eyes and bade them bring shears to cut him loose, for his hair had bound him a fast prisoner, and he could not move. And then he sent them for rich clothes, and jewels, which he put on; and he ordered them to saddle the white horse, with gold and silk, that he might ride to meet the King; but he quite forgot he had a grand-daughter to take to the ball.

Meanwhile Tattercoats sat by the kitchen-door weeping, because she could not go to see the grand doings. And when the old nurse heard her crying she went to the Lord of the Palace, and begged him to take his granddaughter with him to the King's ball.

But he only frowned and told her to be silent; while the servants laughed and said, "Tattercoats is happy in her rags, playing with the gooseherd! Let her be—it is all she is fit for."

A second, and then a third time, the old nurse begged him to let the girl go with him, but she was answered only by black looks and fierce words, till she was driven from the room by the jeering servants, with blows and mocking words.

Weeping over her ill-success, the old nurse went to look for Tattercoats; but the girl had been turned from the door by the cook, and had run away to tell her friend the gooseherd how unhappy she was because she could not go to the King's ball.

Now when the gooseherd had listened to her story, he bade her cheer up, and proposed that they should go together into the town to see the King, and all the fine things; and when she looked sorrowfully down at her rags and bare feet he played a note or two upon his pipe, so gay and merry, that she forgot all about her tears and her troubles and before she well knew, the gooseherd had taken her by the hand, and she and he, and the geese before them, were dancing down the road towards the town.

"Even cripples can dance when they choose," said the gooseherd.

Before they had gone very far a handsome young man, splendidly dressed, riding up, stopped to ask the way to the castle where the King was staying, and when he found that they too were going thither, he got off his horse and walked beside them along the road.

Tattercoats dancing while the gooseherd pipes.

"You seem merry folk," he said, "and will be good company."

"Good company, indeed," said the gooseherd, and played a new tune that was not a dance.

It was a curious tune, and it made the strange young man stare and stare and stare at Tattercoats till he couldn't see her rags—till he couldn't, to tell the truth, see anything but her beautiful face.

Then he said, "You are the most beautiful maiden in the world. Will you marry me?"

Then the gooseherd smiled to himself, and played sweeter than ever.

But Tattercoats laughed. "Not I," said she; "you would be finely put to shame, and so would I be, if you took a goose-girl for your wife! Go and ask one of the great ladies you will see to-night at the King's ball, and do not flout poor Tattercoats."

But the more she refused him the sweeter the pipe played, and the deeper the young man fell in love; till at last he begged her to come that night at twelve to the King's ball, just as she was, with the gooseherd and his geese, in her torn petticoat and bare feet, and see if he wouldn't dance with her before the King and the lords and ladies, and present her to them all, as his dear and honoured bride.

Now at first Tattercoats said she would not; but the gooseherd said, "Take fortune when it comes, little one."

So when night came, and the hall in the castle was full of light and music, and the lords and ladies were dancing before the King, just as the clock struck twelve, Tattercoats and the gooseherd, followed by his flock of noisy geese, hissing and swaying their heads, entered at the great doors, and walked straight up the ball-room, while on either side the ladies whispered, the lords laughed, and the King seated at the far end stared in amazement.

But as they came in front of the throne Tattercoats' lover rose from beside the King, and came to meet her. Taking her by the hand, he kissed her thrice before them all, and turned to the King.

"Father!" he said—for it was the Prince himself—"I have made my choice, and here is my bride, the loveliest girl in all the land, and the sweetest as well!"

Before he had finished speaking, the gooseherd had put his pipe to his lips and played a few notes that sounded like a bird singing far off in the woods; and as he played Tattercoats' rags were changed to shining robes sewn with glittering jewels, a golden crown lay upon her golden hair, and the flock of geese behind her became a crowd of dainty pages, bearing her long train.

And as the King rose to greet her as his daughter the trumpets sounded loudly in honour of the new Princess, and the people outside in the street said to each other:

"Ah! now the Prince has chosen for his wife the loveliest girl in all the land!"

But the gooseherd was never seen again, and no one knew what became of him; while the old lord went home once more to his Palace by the sea, for he could not stay at Court, when he had sworn never to look on his grand-daughter's face.

So there he still sits by his window,—if you could only see him, as you may some day—weeping more bitterly than ever. And his white hair has bound him to the stones, and the river of his tears runs away to the great sea.

THE THREE SILLIES

THE THREE SILLIES

Once upon a time, when folk were not so wise as they are nowadays, there lived a farmer and his wife who had one daughter. And she, being a pretty lass, was courted by the young squire when he came home from his travels.

Now every evening he would stroll over from the Hall to see her and stop to supper in the farm-house, and every evening the daughter would go down into the cellar to draw the cider for supper.

So one evening when she had gone down to draw the cider and had turned the tap as usual, she happened to look up at the ceiling, and there she saw a big wooden mallet stuck in one of the beams.

It must have been there for ages and ages, for it was all covered with cobwebs; but somehow or another she had never noticed it before, and at once she began thinking how dangerous it was to have the mallet just there.

"For," thought she, "supposing him and me was married, and supposing we was to have a son, and supposing he were to grow up to be a man, and supposing he were to come down to draw cider like as I'm doing, and supposing the mallet were to fall on his head and kill him, how dreadful it would be!"

And with that she put down the candle she was carrying and, seating herself on a cask, began to cry. And she cried and cried and cried.

Now, upstairs, they began to wonder why she was so long drawing the cider; so after a time her mother went down to the cellar to see what had come to her, and found her, seated on the cask, crying ever so hard, and the cider running all over the floor.

"Lawks a mercy me!" cried her mother, "whatever is the matter?"

"O mother!" says she between her sobs, "it's that horrid mallet. Supposing him and me was married, and supposing we was to have a son, and supposing he was to come down to draw cider like as I'm doing, and supposing the

mallet were to fall on his head and kill him, how dreadful it would be!"

"Dear heart!" said the mother, seating herself beside her daughter and beginning to cry: "How dreadful it would be!"

So they both sat a-crying.

Now after a time, when they did not come back, the farmer began to wonder what had happened, and going down to the cellar found them seated side by side on the cask, crying hard, and the cider running all over the floor.

"Zounds!" says he, "whatever is the matter?"

"Just look at that horrid mallet up there, father," moaned the mother. "Supposing our daughter was to marry her sweetheart, and supposing they was to have a son, and supposing he was to grow to man's estate, and supposing he was to come down to draw cider like as we're doing, and supposing that there mallet was to fall on his head and kill him, how dreadful it would be!"

"Dreadful indeed!" said the father and, seating himself beside his wife and daughter, started a-crying too.

Now upstairs the young squire wanted his supper; so at last he lost patience and went down into the cellar to see for himself what they were all after. And there he found them seated side by side on the cask a-crying, with their feet all a-wash in cider, for the floor was fair flooded. So the first thing he did was to run straight and turn off the tap. Then he said:

"What are you three after, sitting there crying like babies, and letting good cider run over the floor?"

Then they all three began with one voice, "Look at that horrid mallet! Supposing you and me—she—was married, and supposing we—you—had a son, and supposing he was to grow to man's estate, and supposing he was to come down here to draw cider like as we be, and supposing that there mallet was to fall down on his head and kill him, how dreadful it would be!"

Then the young squire burst out a-laughing, and laughed till he was tired. But at last he reached up to the old mallet and pulled it out, and put it safe on the floor. And he shook his head and said, "I've travelled far and I've travelled fast, but never have I met with three such sillies as you three. Now I can't marry one of the three biggest sillies in the world. So I shall start again on my travels, and if I can find three bigger sillies than you three, then I'll come back and be married—not otherwise."

So he wished them good-bye and started again on his travels, leaving them all crying; this time because the marriage was off!

Well, the young man travelled far and he travelled fast, but never did he find a bigger silly, until one day he came upon an old woman's cottage that had some grass growing on the thatched roof.

And the old woman was trying her best to cudgel her cow into going up a ladder to eat the grass. But the poor thing was afraid and durst not go. Then the old woman tried coaxing, but it wouldn't go. You never saw such a sight! The cow getting more and more flustered and obstinate, the old woman getting hotter and hotter.

At last the young squire said, "It would be easier if *you* went up the ladder, cut the grass, and threw it down for the cow to eat."

"A likely story that," says the old woman. "A cow can cut grass for herself. And the foolish thing will be quite safe up there, for I'll tie a rope round her neck, pass the rope down the chimney, and fasten t'other end to my wrist, so

71

as when I'm doing my bit o' washing, she can't fall off the roof without my knowing it. So mind your own business, young sir."

Well, after a while the old woman coaxed and codgered and bullied and badgered the cow up the ladder, and when she got it on to the roof she tied a rope round its neck, passed the rope down the chimney, and fastened t'other end to her wrist. Then she went about her bit of washing, and the young squire he went on his way.

But he hadn't gone but a bit when he heard the awfullest hullabaloo. He galloped back, and found that the cow had fallen off the roof and got strangled by the rope round its neck, while the weight of the cow had pulled the old woman by her wrist up the chimney, where she had got stuck half-way and been smothered by the soot!

"That is one bigger silly," quoth the young squire as he journeyed on. "So now for two more!"

He did not find any, however, till late one night he arrived at a little inn. And the inn was so full that he had to share a room with another traveller. Now his room-fellow proved quite a pleasant fellow, and they forgathered, and each slept well in his bed.

But next morning, when they were dressing, what does the stranger do but carefully hang his breeches on the knobs of the tallboy!

"What are you doing?" asks young squire.

"I'm putting on my breeches," says the stranger; and with that he goes to the other end of the room, takes a little run, and tried to jump into the breeches.

But he didn't succeed, so he took another run and another try, and another and another and another, until he got quite hot and flustered, as the old woman had got over her cow that wouldn't go up the ladder. And all the time young squire was laughing fit to split, for never in his life did he see anything so comical.

Then the stranger stopped a while and mopped his face with his handkerchief, for he was all in a sweat. "It's very well laughing," says he, "but breeches are the most awkwardest things to get into that ever were. It takes me the best part of an hour every morning before I get them on. How do you manage yours?"

Then young squire showed him, as well as he could for laughing, how to put on his breeches, and the stranger was ever so grateful and said he never should have thought of that way.

"So that," quoth young squire to himself, "is a second bigger silly." But he travelled far and he travelled fast without finding the third, until one bright night when the moon was shining right overhead he came upon a village. And outside the village was a pond, and round about the pond was a great crowd of villagers. And some had got rakes, and some had got pitchforks, and some had got brooms. And they were as busy as busy, shouting out, and raking, and forking, and sweeping away at the pond.

"What is the matter?" cried young squire, jumping off his horse to help. "Has any one fallen in?"

"Aye! Matter enough," says they. "Can't 'ee see moon's fallen into the pond, an' we can't get her out nohow."

And with that they set to again raking, and forking, and sweeping away. Then the young squire burst out laughing, told them they were fools for their pains, and bade them look up over their heads where the moon was riding broad and full. But they wouldn't, and they wouldn't believe that what they saw in the water was only a reflection. And when he insisted they began to abuse him roundly and threaten to duck him in the pond. So he got on his horse again as quickly as he could, leaving them raking, and forking, and sweeping away; and for all we know they may be at it yet!

But the young squire said to himself, "There are many more sillies in this world than I thought for; so I'll just go back and marry the farmer's daughter. She is no sillier than the rest."

So they were married, and if they didn't live happy ever after, that has nothing to do with the story of the three sillies.

HOW JACK WENT OUT TO SEEK HIS FORTUNE

HOW JACK WENT OUT TO SEEK HIS FORTUNE

Once on a time there was a boy named Jack, and one morning he started to go and seek his fortune.

He hadn't gone very far before he met a cat.

"Where are you going, Jack?" said the cat.

"I am going to seek my fortune."

"May I go with you?"

"Yes," said Jack, "the more the merrier."

So on they went, Jack and the cat. Jiggelty-jolt, jiggelty-jolt, jiggelty-jolt!

They went a little farther and they met a dog.

"Where are you going, Jack?" said the dog.

"I am going to seek my fortune."

"May I go with you?"

"Yes," said Jack, "the more the merrier!"

So on they went, Jack, the cat, and the dog! Jiggelty-jolt, jiggelty-jolt, jiggelty-jolt!

They went a little farther and they met a goat.

"Where are you going, Jack?" said the goat.

"I am going to seek my fortune."

"May I go with you?"

"Yes," said Jack, "the more the merrier."

So on they went, Jack, the cat, the dog, and the goat. Jiggelty-jolt, jiggelty-jolt, jiggelty-jolt!

They went a little farther and they met a bull.

"Where are you going, Jack?" said the bull.

"I am going to seek my fortune."

"May I go with you?"

"Yes," said Jack, "the more the merrier."

JIGGELTY-JOLT

So on they went, Jack, the cat, the dog, the goat, and the bull. Jiggelty-jolt, jiggelty-jolt, jiggelty-jolt!

They went a little farther and they met a rooster.

"Where are you going, Jack?" said the rooster.

"I am going to seek my fortune."

"May I go with you?"

"Yes," said Jack, "the more the merrier."

So on they went, Jack, the cat, the dog, the goat, the bull, and the rooster. Jiggelty-jolt, jiggelty-jolt, jiggelty-jolt!

And they went on jiggelty-jolting till it was about dark, and it was time to think of some place where they could spend the night. Now, after a bit, they came in sight of a house, and Jack told his companions to keep still while he went up and looked in through the window to see if all was safe. And what did he see through the window but a band of robbers seated at a table counting over great bags of gold!

"That gold shall be mine," quoth Jack to himself. "I have found my fortune already."

Then he went back and told his companions to wait till he gave the word, and then to make all the noise they possibly could in their own fashion. So when they were all ready Jack gave the word, and the cat mewed, and the dog barked, and the goat bleated, and the bull bellowed, and the rooster crowed, and all together they made such a terrific hubbub that the robbers jumped up in a fright and ran away, leaving their gold on the table. So, after a good laugh, Jack and his companions went in and took possession of the house and the gold.

Now Jack was a wise boy, and he knew that the robbers would come back in the dead of the night to get their gold, and so when it came time to go to bed he put the cat in the rocking-chair, and he put the dog under the table, and he put the goat upstairs, and he put the bull in the cellar, and bade the rooster fly up on to the roof.

Then he went to bed.

Now sure enough, in the dead of the night, the robbers sent one man back to the house to look after their money. But before long he came back in a great fright and told them a fearsome tale!

"I went back to the house," said he, "and went in and tried to sit down in the rocking-chair, and there was an old woman knitting there, and she—oh my!—stuck her knitting-needles into me."

(*That was the cat, you know.*)

"Then I went to the table to look after the money, but there was a shoemaker under the table, and my! how he stuck his awl into me."

(*That was the dog, you know.*)

"So I started to go upstairs, but there was a man up there threshing, and goody! how he knocked me down with the flail!"

(*That was the goat, you know.*)

"Then I started to go down to the cellar, but—oh dear me!—there was a man down there chopping wood, and he knocked me up and he knocked me down just terrible with his axe."

(*That was the bull, you know.*)

"But I shouldn't have minded all that if it hadn't been for an awful little fellow on the top of the house by the kitchen chimney, who kept a-hollering and hollering, 'Cook him in a stew! Cook him in a stew! Cook him in a stew!'"

(*And that, of course, was the cock-a-doodle-doo.*)

Then the robbers agreed that they would rather lose their gold than meet with such a fate; so they made off, and Jack next morning went gaily home with his booty. And each of the animals carried a portion of it. The cat hung a bag on its tail (a cat when it walks always carries its tail stiff), the dog on his collar, the goat and the bull on their horns, but Jack made the rooster carry a golden guinea in its beak to prevent it from calling all the time:

"Cock-a-doodle-doo,
Cook him in a stew!"

DICK WHITTINGTON
AND HIS CAT

DICK WHITTINGTON
AND HIS CAT

More than five hundred years ago there was a little boy named Dick Whittington, and this is true. His father and mother died when he was too young to work, and so poor little Dick was very badly off. He was quite glad to get the parings of the potatoes to eat and a dry crust of bread now and then, and more than that he did not often get, for the village where he lived was a very poor one and the neighbours were not able to spare him much.

Now the country folk in those days thought that the people of London were all fine ladies and gentlemen, and that there was singing and dancing all the day long, and so rich were they there that even the streets, they said, were paved with gold. Dick used to sit by and listen while all these strange tales of the wealth of London were told, and it made him long to go and live there and have plenty to eat and fine clothes to wear, instead of the rags and hard fare that fell to his lot in the country.

So one day when a great wagon with eight horses stopped on its way through the village, Dick made friends with the waggoner and begged to be taken with him to London. The man felt sorry for poor little Dick when he heard that he had no father or mother to take care of him, and saw how ragged and how badly in need of help he was. So he agreed to take him, and off they set.

How far it was and how many days they took over the journey I do not know, but in due time Dick found himself in the wonderful city which he had heard so much of and pictured to himself so grandly. But oh! how disappointed he was when he got there. How dirty it was! And the people, how unlike the gay company, with music and singing, that he had dreamt of! He wandered up and down the streets, one after another, until he was tired out, but not one did he find that was paved with gold. Dirt in plenty he could see, but none of the gold that he thought to have put in his pockets as fast as he chose to pick it up.

Little Dick ran about till he was tired and it was growing dark. And at last he sat himself down in a corner and fell asleep. When morning came he was very cold and hungry, and though he asked every one he met to help him, only one or two gave him a halfpenny to buy some bread. For two or three days he lived in the streets in this way, only just able to keep himself alive, when he managed to get some work to do in a hayfield, and that kept him for a short time longer, till the haymaking was over.

After this he was as badly off as ever, and did not know where to turn. one day in his wanderings he lay down to rest in the doorway of the house of a rich merchant whose name was Fitzwarren. But here he was soon seen by the cook-maid, who was an unkind, bad-tempered woman, and she cried out to him to be off. "Lazy rogue," she called him; and she said she'd precious quick throw some dirty dishwater over him, boiling hot, if he didn't go. However, just then Mr. Fitzwarren himself came home to dinner, and when he saw what was happening, he asked Dick why he was lying there. "You're old enough to be at work, my boy," he said. "I'm afraid you have a mind to be lazy."

"Indeed, sir," said Dick to him, "indeed that is not so"; and he told him how hard he had tried to get work to do, and how ill he was for want of food. Dick, poor fellow, was now so weak that though he tried to stand he had to lie down again, for it was more than three days since he had had anything to eat at all. The kind merchant gave orders for him to be taken into the house and gave him a good dinner, and then he said that he was to be kept, to do what work he could to help the cook.

Many's the beating he had from the broomstick or the ladle.

And now Dick would have been happy enough in this good family if it had not been for the ill-natured cook, who did her best to make life a burden to him. Night and morning she was for ever scolding him. Nothing he did was good enough. It was "Look sharp here" and "Hurry up there," and there was no pleasing her. And many's the beating he had from the broomstick or the ladle, or whatever else she had in her hand.

At last it came to the ears of Miss Alice, Mr. Fitzwarren's daughter, how badly the cook was treating poor Dick. And she told the cook that she would quickly lose her place if she didn't treat him more kindly, for Dick had become quite a favourite with the family.

After that the cook's behaviour was a little better, but Dick still had another hardship that he bore with difficulty. For he slept in a garret where were so many holes in the walls and the floor that every night as he lay in bed the room was overrun with rats and mice, and sometimes he could hardly sleep a wink. One day when he had earned a penny for cleaning a gentleman's shoes, he met a little girl with a cat in her arms, and asked whether she would not sell it to him. "Yes, she would," she said, though the cat was such a good mouser that she was sorry to part with her. This just suited Dick, who kept pussy up in his garret, feeding her on scraps of his own dinner that he saved for her every day. In a little while he had no more bother with the rats and mice. Puss soon saw to that, and he slept sound every night.

Soon after this Mr. Fitzwarren had a ship ready to sail; and as it was his custom that all his servants should be given a chance of good fortune as well as himself, he called them all into the counting-house and asked them what they would send out.

They all had something that they were willing to venture except poor Dick, who had neither money nor goods, and so could send nothing. For this reason he did not come into the room with the rest. But Miss Alice guessed what was the matter, and ordered him to be called in. She then said, "I will lay down some money for him out of my own purse"; but her father told her that would not do, for it must be something of his own.

When Dick heard this he said, "I have nothing whatever but a cat, which I bought for a penny some time ago."

"Go, my boy, fetch your cat then," said his master, "and let her go."

Dick went upstairs and fetched poor puss, but there were tears in his eyes when he gave her to the captain. "For," he said, "I shall now be kept awake all night by the rats and mice." All the company laughed at Dick's odd venture, and Miss Alice, who felt sorry for him, gave him some money to buy another cat.

Now this, and other marks of kindness shown him by Miss Alice, made the ill-tempered cook jealous of poor Dick, and she began to use him more cruelly than ever, and was always making game of him for sending his cat to sea. "What do you think your cat will sell for?" she'd ask. "As much money as would buy a stick to beat you with?"

At last poor Dick could not bear this usage any longer, and he thought he would run away. So he made a bundle of his things—he hadn't many—and started very early in the morning, on All-Hallows' Day, the first of November. He walked as far as Holloway, and there he sat down to rest on a stone, which to this day, they say, is called "Whittington's Stone," and began to wonder to himself which road he should take.

When Puss saw the rats and mice she didn't wait to be told.

While he was thinking what he should do, the bells of Bow Church in Cheapside began to chime, and as they rang he fancied that they were singing over and over again:

"Turn again, Whittington,
Lord Mayor of London."

"Lord Mayor of London!" said he to himself. "Why, to be sure, wouldn't I put up with almost anything now to be Lord Mayor of London, and ride in a fine coach, when I grow to be a man! Well, I'll go back, and think nothing of the cuffing and scolding of the cross old cook if I am to be Lord Mayor of London at last."

So back he went, and he was lucky enough to get into the house and set about his work before the cook came down.

But now you must hear what befell Mrs. Puss all this while. The ship *Unicorn* that she was on was a long time at sea, and the cat made herself useful, as she would, among the unwelcome rats that lived on board too. At last the ship put into harbour on the coast of Barbary, where the only people are the Moors. They had never before seen a ship from England, and flocked in numbers to see the sailors, whose different colour and foreign dress were a great wonder to them. They were soon eager to buy the goods with which the ship was laden, and patterns were sent ashore for the King to see. He was so much pleased with them that he sent for the captain to come to the palace, and honoured him with an invitation to dinner. But no sooner were they seated, as is the custom there, on the fine rugs and carpets that covered the floor, than great numbers of rats and mice came scampering in, swarming over all the dishes, and helping themselves from all the good things there were to eat. The captain was amazed, and wondered whether they didn't find such a pest most unpleasant.

"Oh yes," said they, "it was so, and the King would give half his treasure to be freed of them, for they not only spoil his dinner, but they even attack him in his bed at night, so that a watch has to be kept while he is sleeping, for fear of them."

The captain was overjoyed; he thought at once of poor Dick Whittington and his cat, and said he had a creature on board ship that would soon do for all these vermin if she were there. Of course, when the King heard this he was eager to possess this wonderful animal.

"Bring it to me at once," he said; "for the vermin are dreadful, and if only it will do what you say, I will load your ship with gold and jewels in exchange for it."

The captain, who knew his business, took care not to underrate the value of Dick's cat. He told His Majesty how inconvenient it would be to part with her, as when she was gone the rats might destroy the goods in the ship; however, to oblige the King, he would fetch her.

"Oh, make haste, do!" cried the Queen; "I, too, am all impatience to see this dear creature."

Off went the captain, while another dinner was got ready. He took Puss under his arm and got back to the palace just in time to see the carpet covered with rats and mice once again. When Puss saw them she didn't wait to be told, but jumped out of the captain's arms, and in no time almost all the rats and mice were dead at her feet, while the rest of them had scuttled off to their holes in fright.

The King was delighted to get rid so easily of such an intolerable plague, and the Queen desired that the animal who had done them such a service might be brought to her. Upon which the captain called out, "Puss, puss, puss," and she came running to him. Then he presented her to the Queen, who was rather afraid at first to touch a creature who had made such a havoc with her claws. However, when the captain called her, "Pussy, pussy," and began to stroke her, the Queen also ventured to touch her and cried, "Putty, putty," in imitation of the captain, for she hadn't learned to speak English. He then put her on to the Queen's lap, where she purred and played with Her Majesty's hand and was soon asleep.

The King having seen what Mrs. Puss could do, and learning that her kittens would soon stock the whole country, and keep it free from rats, after bargaining with the captain for the whole ship's cargo, then gave him ten times as much for the cat as all the rest amounted to.

The captain then said farewell to the court of Barbary, and after a fair voyage reached London again with his precious load of gold and jewels safe and sound.

One morning early Mr. Fitzwilliam had just come to his counting-house and settled himself at the desk to count the cash, when there came a knock at the door. "Who's there?" said he. "A friend," replied a voice. "I come with good news of your ship the *Unicorn*." The merchant in haste opened the door, and who were there but the ship's captain and the mate, bearing a chest of jewels and a bill of lading. When he had looked this over he lifted his eyes and thanked heaven for sending him such a prosperous voyage.

The honest captain next told him all about the cat, and showed him the rich present the King had sent for her to poor Dick. Rejoicing on behalf of Dick as much as he had done over his own good fortune, he called out to his servants to come and to bring up Dick:

"Go fetch him, and we'll tell him of his fame;
Pray call him Mr. Whittington by name."

The servants, some of them, hesitated at this, and said so great a treasure was too much for a lad like Dick; but Mr. Fitzwarren now showed himself the good man that he was and refused to deprive him of the value of a single penny. "God forbid!" he cried. "It's all his own, and he shall have it, to a farthing."

He then sent for Dick, who at the moment was scouring pots for the cook and was black with dirt. He tried to excuse himself from coming into the room in such a plight, but the merchant made him come, and had a chair set for him. And he then began to think they must be making game of him, so he begged them not to play tricks on a poor simple boy, but to let him go downstairs again back to his work in the scullery.

"Indeed, Mr. Whittington," said the merchant, "we are all quite in earnest with you, and I most heartily rejoice at the news that these gentlemen have brought. For the captain has sold your cat to the King of Barbary, and brings you in return for her more riches than I possess in the whole world; and may you long enjoy them!"

Mr. Fitzwarren then told the men to open the great treasure they had brought with them, saying, "There is nothing more now for Mr. Whittington to do but to put it in some place of safety."

Poor Dick hardly knew how to behave himself for joy. He begged his master to take what part of it he pleased, since he owed it all to his kindness. "No, no," answered Mr. Fitzwarren, "this all belongs to you; and I have no doubt that you will use it well."

Dick next begged his mistress, and then Miss Alice, to accept a part of his good fortune, but they would not, and at the same time told him what great joy they felt at his great success. But he was far too kind-hearted to keep it all to himself; so he made a present to the captain, the mate, and the rest of Mr. Fitzwarren's servants; and even to his old enemy, the cross cook.

After this Mr. Fitzwarren advised him to send for a tailor and get himself dressed like a gentleman, and told him he was welcome to live in his house till he could provide himself with a better.

When Whittington's face was washed, his hair curled, and he was dressed in a smart suit of clothes, he was just as handsome and fine a young man as any who visited at Mr. Fitzwarren's, and so thought fair Alice Fitzwarren, who had once been so kind to him and looked upon him with pity. And now she felt he was quite fit to be her sweetheart, and none the less, no doubt, because Whittington was always thinking what he could do to please her, and making her the prettiest presents that could be.

Mr. Fitzwarren soon saw which way the wind blew, and ere long proposed to join them in marriage, and to this they both readily agreed. A day for the wedding was soon fixed; and they were attended to church by the Lord Mayor, the court of aldermen, the sheriffs, and a great number of the richest merchants in London, whom they afterwards treated with a magnificent feast.

History tells us that Mr. Whittington and his lady lived in great splendour, and were very happy. They had several children. He was Sheriff, and thrice Lord Mayor of London, and received the honour of knighthood from Henry V.

After the King's conquest of France, Sir Richard Whittington entertained him and the Queen at dinner at the Mansion House in so sumptuous a manner that the King said, "Never had Prince such a subject!" To which Sir Richard replied, "Never had subject such a Prince."

CATSKIN

CATSKIN

Once upon a time there lived a gentleman who owned fine lands and houses, and he very much wanted to have a son to be heir to them. So when his wife brought him a daughter, though she was bonny as bonny could be, he cared nought for her, and said:

"Let me never see her face."

So she grew up to be a beautiful maiden, though her father never set eyes on her till she was fifteen years old and was ready to be married.

Then her father said roughly, "She shall marry the first that comes for her." Now when this became known, who should come along and be first but a nasty, horrid old man! So she didn't know what to do, and went to the hen-wife and asked her advice. And the hen-wife said, "Say you will not take him unless they give you a coat of silver cloth." Well, they gave her a coat of silver cloth, but she wouldn't take him for all that, but went again to the hen-wife, who said, "Say you will not take him unless they give you a coat of beaten gold." Well, they gave her a coat of beaten gold, but still she would not take the old man, but went again to the hen-wife, who said, "Say you will not take him unless they give you a coat made of the feathers of all the birds of the air." So they sent out a man with a great heap of peas; and the man cried to all the birds of the air, "Each bird take a pea and put down a feather." So each bird took a pea and put down one of its feathers: and they took all the feathers and made a coat of them and gave it to her; but still she would not take the nasty, horrid old man, but asked the hen-wife once again what she was to do, and the hen-wife said, "Say they must first make you a coat of catskin." Then they made her a coat of catskin; and she put it on, and tied up her other coats into a bundle, and when it was night-time ran away with it into the woods.

Now she went along, and went along, and went along, till at the end of the wood she saw a fine castle. Then she hid her fine dresses by a crystal waterfall and went up to the castle gates and asked for work. The lady of the castle saw her, and told her, "I'm sorry I have no better place, but if you like you may be our scullion." So down she went into the kitchen, and they called her Catskin, because of her dress. But the cook was very cruel to her, and led her a sad life.

Well, soon after that it happened that the young lord of the castle came home, and there was to be a grand ball in honour of the occasion. And when they were speaking about it among the servants, "Dear me, Mrs. Cook," said Catskin, "how much I should like to go!"

"What! You dirty, impudent slut," said the cook, "you go among all the fine lords and ladies with your filthy catskin? A fine figure you'd cut!" and with that she took a basin of water and dashed it into Catskin's face. But Catskin only shook her ears and said nothing.

Now when the day of the ball arrived, Catskin slipped out of the house and went to the edge of the forest where she had hidden her dresses. Then she bathed herself in a crystal waterfall, and put on her coat of silver cloth, and hastened away to the ball. As soon as she entered all were overcome by her beauty and grace, while the young lord at once lost his heart to her. He asked her to be his partner for the first dance; and he would dance with none other the livelong night.

When it came to parting time, the young lord said, "Pray tell me, fair maid, where you live?"

But Catskin curtsied and said:

"Kind sir, if the truth I must tell,
At the sign of the 'Basin of Water' I dwell."

Then she flew from the castle and donned her catskin robe again, and slipped into the scullery, unbeknown to the cook.

The young lord went the very next day and searched for the sign of the "Basin of Water"; but he could not find it. So he went to his mother, the lady of the castle, and declared he would wed none other but the lady of the silver dress, and would never rest till he had found her. So another ball was soon arranged in hopes that the beautiful maid would appear again.

So Catskin said to the cook, "Oh, how I should like to go!" Whereupon the cook screamed out in a rage, "What you, you dirty, im-

She went along, and went along, and went along.

pudent slut! You would cut a fine figure among all the fine lords and ladies." And with that she up with a ladle and broke it across Catskin's back. But Catskin only shook her ears, and ran off to the forest, where, first of all, she bathed, and then she put on her coat of beaten gold, and off she went to the ball-room.

As soon as she entered all eyes were upon her; and the young lord at once recognized her as the lady of the "Basin of Water," claimed her hand for the first dance, and did not leave her till the last. When that came, he again asked her where she lived. But all that she would say was:

> "Kind sir, if the truth I must tell,
> At the sign of the 'Broken Ladle' I dwell";

and with that she curtsied and flew from the ball, off with her golden robe, on with her catskin, and into the scullery without the cook's knowing.

Next day, when the young lord could not find where the sign of the "Basin of Water" was, he begged his mother to have another grand ball, so that he might meet the beautiful maid once more.

Then Catskin said to the cook, "Oh, how I wish I could go to the ball!" Whereupon the cook called out: "A fine figure you'd cut!" and broke the skimmer across her head. But Catskin only shook her ears, and went off to the forest, where she first bathed in the crystal spring, and then donned her coat of feathers, and so off to the ball-room.

When she entered every one was surprised at so beautiful a face and form dressed in so rich and rare a dress; but the young lord at once recognized his beautiful sweetheart, and would dance with none but her the whole evening. When the ball came to an end he pressed her to tell him where she lived, but all she would answer was:

> "Kind sir, if the truth I must tell,
> At the sign of the 'Broken Skimmer' I dwell";

and with that she curtsied, and was off to the forest. But this time the young lord followed her, and watched her change her fine dress of feathers for her catskin dress, and then he knew her for his own scullery-maid.

Next day he went to his mother, and told her that he wished to marry the scullery-maid, Catskin.

"Never," said the lady of the castle—"never so long as I live."

Well the young lord was so grieved that he took to his bed and was very ill indeed. The doctor tried to cure him, but he would not take any medicine unless from the hands of Catskin. At last the doctor went to the mother, and said that her son would die if she did not consent to his marriage with Catskin; so she had to give way. Then she summoned Catskin to her, and Catskin put on her coat of beaten gold before she went to see the lady; and she, of course, was overcome at once, and was only too glad to wed her son to so beautiful a maid.

So they were married, and after a time a little son was born to them, and grew up a fine little lad. Now one day, when he was about four years old, a beggar woman came to the door, and Lady Catskin gave some money to the little lord and told him to go and give it to the beggar woman. So he went and gave it, putting it into the hand of the woman's baby child; and the child leaned forward and kissed the little lord.

Now the wicked old cook (who had never been sent away, because Catskin was too kind-hearted) was looking on, and she said, "See how beggars' brats take to one another!"

This insult hurt Catskin dreadfully: and she went to her husband, the young lord, and told him all about her father, and begged he would go and find out what had become of her parents. So they set out in the lord's grand coach, and travelled through the forest till they came to the house of Catskin's father. Then they put up at an inn near, and Catskin stopped there, while her husband went to see if her father would own she was his daughter.

Now her father had never had any other child, and his wife had died; so he was all alone in the world, and sate moping and miserable. When the young lord came in he hardly looked up, he was so miserable. Then Catskin's husband drew a chair close up to him, and asked him, "Pray, sir, had you not once a young daughter whom you would never see or own?"

And the miserable man said with tears, "It is true; I am a hardened sinner. But I would give all my worldly goods if I could see her once before I die."

Then the young lord told him what had happened to Catskin, and took him to the inn, and afterwards brought his father-in-law to his own castle, where they lived happy ever afterwards.

THE STORY OF
THE THREE BEARS

THE STORY OF THE THREE BEARS

Once upon a time there were three Bears, who lived together in a house of their own, in a wood. One of them was a Little Wee Bear, and one was a Middle-sized Bear, and the other was a Great Big Bear. They had each a bowl for their porridge: a little bowl for the Little Wee Bear; and a middle-sized bowl for the Middle-sized Bear; and a great bowl for the Great Big Bear. And they had each a chair to sit in: a little chair for the Little Wee Bear; and a middle-sized chair for the Middle-sized Bear; and a great chair for the Great Big Bear. And they had each a bed to sleep in: a little bed for the Little Wee Bear; and a middle-sized bed for the Middle-sized Bear; and a great bed for the Great Big Bear.

One day, after they had made the porridge for their breakfast, and poured it into their porridge-bowls, they walked out into the wood while the porridge was cooling, that they might not burn their mouths by beginning too soon, for they were polite, well-brought-up Bears. And while they were away a little girl called Goldilocks, who lived at the other side of the wood and had been sent on an errand by her mother, passed by the house, and looked in at the window. And then she peeped in at the keyhole, for she was not at all a well-brought-up little girl. Then seeing nobody in the house she lifted the latch. The door was not fastened, because the Bears were good Bears, who did nobody any harm, and never suspected that anybody would harm them. So Goldilocks opened the door and went in; and well pleased was she when she saw the porridge on the table. If she had been a well-brought-up little girl she would have waited till the Bears came home, and then, perhaps, they would have asked her to breakfast; for they were good Bears—a little rough or so, as the manner of Bears is, but for all that very good-natured and hospitable. But she was an impudent, rude little girl, and so she set about helping herself.

First she tasted the porridge of the Great Big Bear, and that was too hot for her. Next she tasted the porridge of the Middle-sized Bear, but that was too cold for her. And then she went to the porridge of the Little Wee Bear, and tasted it, and that was neither too hot nor too cold, but just right, and she liked it so well that she ate it all up, every bit!

Then Goldilocks, who was tired, for she had been catching butterflies instead of running her errand, sate down in the chair of the Great Big Bear, but that was too hard for her. And then she sate down in the chair of the Middle-sized Bear, and that was too soft for her. But when she sat down in the chair of the Little Wee Bear, that was neither too hard nor too soft, but just right. So she seated herself in it, and there she sate till the bottom of the chair came out, and down she came, plump upon the ground; and that made her very cross, for she was a bad-tempered little girl.

Now, being determined to rest, Goldilocks went upstairs into the bed-chamber in which the Three Bears slept. And first she lay down upon the bed of the Great Big Bear, but that was too high at the head for her. And next she lay down upon the bed of the Middle-sized Bear, and that was too high at the foot for her. And then she lay down upon the bed of the Little Wee Bear, and that was neither too high at the head nor at the foot, but just right. So she covered herself up comfortably, and lay there till she fell fast asleep.

By this time the Three Bears thought their porridge would be cool enough for them to eat it properly; so thay came home to breakfast. Now careless Goldilocks had left the spoon of the Great Big Bear standing in his porridge.

"SOMEBODY HAS BEEN AT MY PORRIDGE!"

said the Great Big Bear in his great, rough, gruff voice.

Then the Middle-sized Bear looked at his porridge and saw the spoon was standing in it too.

"SOMEBODY HAS BEEN AT MY PORRIDGE!"

said the Middle-sized Bear in his middle-sized voice.

Then the Little Wee Bear looked at his, and there was the spoon in the porridge-bowl, but the porridge was all gone!

"SOMEBODY HAS BEEN AT MY PORRIDGE, AND HAS EATEN IT ALL UP!"

"Somebody has been at my porridge, and has eaten it all up!"

said the Little Wee Bear in his little wee voice.

Upon this the Three Bears, seeing that some one had entered their house, and eaten up the Little Wee Bear's breakfast, began to look about them. Now the careless Goldilocks had not put the hard cushion straight when she rose from the chair of the Great Big Bear.

"SOMEBODY HAS BEEN SITTING IN MY CHAIR!"

said the Great Big Bear in his great, rough, gruff voice.

And the careless Goldilocks had squatted down the soft cushion of the Middle-sized Bear.

"SOMEBODY HAS BEEN SITTING IN MY CHAIR!"

said the Middle-sized Bear in his middle-sized voice.

"SOMEBODY HAS BEEN SITTING IN MY CHAIR, AND HAS SATE THE BOTTOM THROUGH!"

said the Little Wee Bear in his little wee voice.

Then the Three Bears thought they had better make further search in case it was a burglar, so they went upstairs into their bedchamber. Now Goldilocks had pulled the pillow of the Great Big Bear out of its place.

"SOMEBODY HAS BEEN LYING IN MY BED!"

said the Great Big Bear in his great, rough, gruff voice.

And Goldilocks had pulled the bolster of the Middle-sized Bear out of its place.

"SOMEBODY HAS BEEN LYING IN MY BED!"

said the Middle-sized Bear in his middle-sized voice.

But when the Little Wee Bear came to look at his bed, there was the bolster in its place!

And the pillow was in its place upon the bolster!

And upon the pillow_____?

There was Goldilocks' yellow head—which was not in its place, for she had no business there.

"SOMEBODY HAS BEEN LYING IN MY BED, – AND HERE SHE IS STILL!"

said the Little Wee Bear in his little wee voice.

Now Goldilocks had heard in her sleep the great, rough, gruff voice of the Great Big Bear; but she was so fast asleep that it was no more to her than the roaring of wind, or the rumbling of thunder. And she had heard the middle-sized voice of the Middle-sized Bear, but it was only as if she had heard some one speaking in a dream. But when she heard the little wee voice of the Little Wee Bear, it was so sharp, and so shrill, that it awakened her at once. Up she started, and when she saw the Three Bears on one side of the bed, she tumbled herself out at the other, and ran to the window. Now the window was open, because the Bears, like good, tidy Bears, as they were, always opened their bedchamber window when they got up in the morning. So naughty, frightened little Goldilocks jumped; and whether she broke her neck in the fall, or ran into the wood and was lost there, or found her way out of the wood and got whipped for being a bad girl and playing truant, no one can say. But the Three Bears never saw anything more of her.

THE TRUE HISTORY
OF
SIR THOMAS THUMB

THE TRUE HISTORY OF SIR THOMAS THUMB

At the court of great King Arthur, who lived, as all know, when knights were bold, and ladies were fair indeed, one of the most renowned of men was the wizard Merlin. Never before or since was there such another. All that was to be known of wizardry he knew, and his advice was ever good and kindly.

Now once when he was travelling in the guise of a beggar, he chanced upon an honest ploughman and his wife who, giving him a hearty welcome, supplied him, cheerfully, with a big wooden bowl of fresh milk and some coarse brown bread on a wooden platter. Still, though both they and the little cottage where they dwelt were neat and tidy, Merlin noticed that neither the husband nor the wife seemed happy; and when he asked the cause they said it was because they had no children.

"Had I but a son, no matter if he were no bigger than my goodman's thumb," said the poor woman, "we should be quite content."

Now this idea of a boy no bigger than a man's thumb so tickled Wizard Merlin's fancy that he promised straight away that such a son should come in due time to bring the good couple content. This done, he went off at once to pay a visit to the Queen of the Fairies, since he felt that the little people would best be able to carry out his promise. And, sure enough, the droll fancy of a mannikin no bigger than his father's thumb tickled the Fairy Queen also, and she set about the task at once.

So behold the ploughman and his wife as happy as King and Queen over the tiniest of tiny babes; and all the happier because the Fairy Queen, anxious to see the little fellow, flew in at the window, bringing with her clothes fit for the wee mannikin to wear.

An oak-leaf hat he had for his crown;
His jacket was woven of thistle-down.
His shirt was a web by spiders spun;
His breeches of softest feathers were done.
His stockings of red-apple rind were tyne
With an eyelash plucked from his mother's eyne.
His shoes were made of a mouse's skin,
Tanned with the soft furry hair within.

Dressed in this guise he looked the prettiest little fellow ever seen, and the Fairy Queen kissed him over and over again, and gave him the name of Tom Thumb.

Now as he grew older—though, mind you, he never grew bigger—he was so full of antics and tricks that he was for ever getting into trouble. Once his mother was making a batter pudding, and Tom, wanting to see how it was made, climbed up to the edge of the bowl. His mother was so busy beating the batter that she didn't notice him; and when his foot slipped, and he plumped head and ears into the bowl, she just went on beating until the batter was light enough. Then she put it into the pudding-cloth and set it on the fire to boil.

Now the batter had so filled poor Tom's mouth that he couldn't cry; but no sooner did he feel the hot water than he begun to struggle and kick so much that the pudding bobbed up and down, and jumped about in such strange fashion that the ploughman's wife thought it was bewitched, and in a great fright flung it to the door.

Here a poor tinker passing by picked it up and put it in his wallet. But by this time Tom had got his mouth clear of the batter, and he began holloaing, and making such a to-do, that the tinker, even more frightened than Tom's mother had been, threw the pudding in the road, and ran away as fast as he could run. Luckily for Tom, this second fall broke the pudding string and he was able to creep out, all covered with half-cooked batter, and make his way home, where his mother, distressed to see her little dear in such a woeful state, put him into a teacup of water to clean him, and then tucked him up in bed.

Another time Tom's mother went to milk her red cow in the meadow and took Tom with her, for she was ever afraid lest he should fall into mischief when left alone. Now the wind was high, and fearful lest he should be blown away, she tied him to a thistle-head with one of her own long hairs, and then began to milk. But the red cow, nosing about for something to do while she was being milked, as all cows will, spied Tom's oak-leaf hat, and thinking it looked good, curled its tongue round the thistle-stalk and——

There was Tom dodging the cow's teeth, and roaring as loud as he could: "Mother! Mother! Help! Help!"

"Lawks-a-mercy-me," cried his mother, "where's the child got to now? Where are you, you bad boy?"

"Here!" roared Tom, "in the red cow's mouth!"

With that his mother began to weep and wail, not knowing what else to do; and Tom, hearing her, roared louder than ever. Whereat the red cow, alarmed—and no wonder!—at the dreadful noise in her throat, opened her mouth, and Tom dropped out, luckily into his mother's apron; otherwise he would have been badly hurt falling so far.

Adventures like these were not Tom's fault. He could not help being so small, but he got into dreadful trouble once for which he was entirely to blame. This is what happened. He loved playing cherry-stones with the big boys, and when he had lost all his own he would creep unbeknownst into the other players' pockets or bags, and make off with cherry-stones enough and galore to carry on the game!

Now one day it so happened that one of the boys saw Master Tom on the point of coming out of a bag with a whole fistful of cherry-stones. So he just drew the string of the bag tight.

"Ha! ha! Mr. Thomas Thumb," says he jeeringly, "so you were going to pinch my cherry-stones, were you? Well! you shall have more of them than you like." And with that he gave the cherry-stone bag such a hearty shake that all Tom's body and legs were sadly bruised black and blue; nor was he let out till he had promised never to steal cherry-stones again.

So the years passed, and when Tom was a lad, still no bigger than a thumb, his father thought he might begin to make himself useful. So he made him a whip out of a barley straw, and set him to drive the cattle home. But Tom, in trying to climb a furrow's ridge—which to him, of course, was a steep hill—slipped down and lay half stunned, so that a raven, happening to fly over, thought he was a frog, and picked him up intending to eat him. Not relishing the morsel, however, the bird dropped him above the battlements of a big castle that stood close to the sea. Now the castle belonged to one Grumbo, an ill-tempered giant who happened to be taking the air on the roof of his tower. And when Tom dropped on his bald pate the giant put up his great hand to catch what he thought was an impudent fly, and finding something that smelt man's meat, he just swallowed the little fellow as he would have swallowed a pill!

He began, however, to repent very soon, for Tom kicked and struggled in the giant's inside as he had done in the red cow's throat until the giant felt quite squeamish, and finally got rid of Tom by being sick over the battlements into the sea.

And here, doubtless, would have been Tom Thumb's end by drowning, had not a big fish, thinking that he was a shrimp, rushed at him and gulped him down!

Now by good chance some fishermen were standing by with their nets, and when they drew them in, the fish that had swallowed Tom was one of the haul. Being a very fine fish it was sent to the Court kitchen, where, when the fish was opened, out popped Tom on the dresser, as spry as spry, to the astonishment of the cook and the scullions! Never had such a mite of a man been seen, while his quips and pranks kept the whole buttery in roars of laughter. What is more, he soon became the favourite of the whole Court, and when the King went out a-riding Tom sat in the Royal waistcoat pocket ready to amuse Royalty and the Knights of the Round Table.

After a while, however, Tom wearied to see his parents again; so the King gave him leave to go home and take with him as much money as he could carry. Tom therefore chose a threepenny bit, and putting it into a purse made of a water bubble, lifted it with difficulty on to his back, and trudged away to his father's house, which was some half a mile distant.

It took him two days and two nights to cover the ground, and he was fair outwearied by his heavy burden ere he reached home. However, his mother put him to rest in a walnut shell by the fire and gave him a whole hazel nut to eat; which, sad to say, disagreed with him dreadfully. However, he recovered in some measure, but had grown so thin and light that to save him the trouble of walking back to the Court, his mother tied him to a dandelion-clock, and as there was a high wind, away he went as if on wings. Unfortunately, however, just as he was flying low in order to alight, the Court cook, an ill-natured fellow, was coming across the palace yard with a bowl of hot furmenty for the King's supper. Now Tom was unskilled in the handling of dandelion horses, so what should happen but that he rode straight into the furmenty, spilt the half of it, and splashed the other half, scalding hot, into the cook's face.

He was in a fine rage, and going straight to King Arthur said that Tom, at his old antics, had done it on purpose.

Now the King's favourite dish was hot furmenty; so he also fell into a fine rage and ordered Tom to be tried for high treason. He was therefore imprisoned in a mouse-trap, where he remained for several days tormented by a cat, who, thinking him some new kind of mouse, spent its time in sparring at him through the bars. At the end of a week, however, King Arthur, having recovered from the loss of the furmenty, sent for Tom and once more received him into favour. After this Tom's life was happy and successful. He became so renowned for his dexterity and wonderful activity, that he was knighted by the King under the name of Sir Thomas Thumb, and as his clothes, what with the batter and the furmenty, to say nothing of the insides of giants and fishes, had become somewhat shabby, His Majesty ordered him a new suit of clothes fit for a mounted knight to wear. He also gave him a beautiful prancing grey mouse as a charger.

It was certainly very diverting to see Tom dressed up to the nines, and as proud as Punch.

> Of butterflies' wings his shirt was made,
> His boots of chicken hide,
> And by a nimble fairy blade,
> All learned in the tailoring trade,
> His coat was well supplied.
> A needle dangled at his side,
> And thus attired in stately pride
> A dapper mouse he used to ride.

In truth the King and all the Knights of the Round Table were ready to expire with laughter at Tom on his fine curveting steed.

But one day, as the hunt was passing a farm-house, a big cat, lurking about, made one spring and carried both Tom and the mouse up a tree. Nothing daunted, Tom boldly drew his needle sword and attacked the enemy with such fierceness that she let her prey fall. Luckily one of the nobles caught the little fellow in his cap, otherwise he must have been killed by the fall. As it was he became very ill, and the doctor almost despaired of his life. However, his friend and guardian, the Queen of the Fairies, arrived in a chariot drawn by flying mice, and then and there carried Tom back with her to Fairyland, where, amongst folk of his own size, he, after a time, recovered. But time runs swiftly in Fairyland, and when Tom Thumb returned to Court he was surprised to find that his father and mother and nearly all his old friends were dead, and that King Thunstone reigned in King Arthur's place. So every one was astonished at his size, and carried him as a curiosity to the Audience Hall.

"Who art thou, mannikin?" asked King Thunstone. "Whence dost come? And where dost live?"

To which Tom replied with a bow:

"My name is well known.
From the Fairies I come.
When King Arthur shone,
This Court was my home.
By him I was knighted,
In me he delighted
—Your servant—Sir Thomas Thumb."

This address so pleased His Majesty that he ordered a little golden chair to be made, so that Tom might sit beside him at table. Also a little palace of gold, but a span high, with doors a bare inch wide, in which the little fellow might take his ease.

Now King Thunstone's Queen was a very jealous woman, and could not bear to see such honours showered on the little fellow; so she up and told the King all sorts of bad tales about his favourite; amongst others, that he had been saucy and rude to her.

Whereupon the King sent for Tom; but forewarned is forearmed, and knowing by bitter experience the danger of royal displeasure, Tom hid himself in an empty snail-shell, where he lay till he was nigh starved. Then seeing a fine large butterfly on a dandelion close by, he climbed up and managed to get astride it. No sooner had he gained his seat than the butterfly was off, hovering from tree to tree, from flower to flower.

At last the royal gardener saw it and gave chase, then the nobles joined in the hunt, even the King himself, and finally the Queen, who forgot her anger in the merriment. Hither and thither they ran, trying in vain to catch the pair, and almost expiring with laughter, until poor Tom, dizzy with so much fluttering, and doubling, and flittering, fell from his seat into a watering-pot, where he was nearly drowned.

So they all agreed he must be forgiven, because he had afforded them so much amusement.

Thus Tom was once more in favour; but he did not live long to enjoy his good luck, for a spider one day attacked him, and though he fought well, the creature's poisonous breath proved too much for him; he fell dead on the ground where he stood, and the spider soon sucked every drop of his blood.

Thus ended Sir Thomas Thumb; but the King and the Court were so sorry at the loss of their little favourite that they went into mourning for him. And they put a fine white marble monument over his grave whereon was carven the following epitaph:

Here lyes Tom Thumb, King Arthur's Knight,
Who died by a spider's fell despite.
He was well known in Arthur's Court,
Where he afforded gallant sport.
He rode at tilt and tournament,
And on a mouse a-hunting went.
Alive he filled the Court with mirth,
His death to sadness must give birth.
So wipe your eyes and shake your head,
And say, "Alas, Tom Thumb is dead!"

JACK AND
THE BEANSTALK

JACK AND THE BEANSTALK

A long long time ago, when most of the world was young and folk did what they liked because all things were good, there lived a boy called Jack.

His father was bed-ridden, and his mother, a good soul, was busy early morns and late eves planning and placing how to support her sick husband and her young son by selling the milk and butter which Milky-White, the beautiful cow, gave them without stint. For it was summer-time. But winter came on; the herbs of the fields took refuge from the frosts in the warm earth, and though his mother sent Jack to gather what fodder he could get in the hedge-rows, he came back as often as not with a very empty sack; for Jack's eyes were so often full of wonder at all the things he saw that sometimes he forgot to work!

So it came to pass that one morning Milky-White gave no milk at all—not one drain! Then the good hard-working mother threw her apron over her head and sobbed:

"What shall we do? What shall we do?"

Now Jack loved his mother; besides, he felt just a bit sneaky at being such a big boy and doing so little to help, so he said, "Cheer up! Cheer up! I'll go and get work somewhere." And he felt as he spoke as if he would work his fingers to the bone; but the good woman shook her head mournfully.

"You've tried that before, Jack," she said, "and nobody would keep you. You are quite a good lad but your wits go a-wool-gathering. No, we must sell Milky-White and live on the money. It is no use crying over milk that is not here to spill!"

You see, she was a wise as well as a hard-working woman, and Jack's spirits rose.

"Just so," he cried. "We will sell Milky-White and be richer than ever. It's an ill wind that blows no one good. So, as it is market-day, I'll just take her there and we shall see what we shall see."

"But——" began his mother.

"But doesn't butter parsnips," laughed Jack. "Trust me to make a good bargain."

So, as it was washing-day, and her sick husband was more ailing than usual, his mother let Jack set off to sell the cow.

"Not less than ten pounds," she bawled after him as he turned the corner.

Ten pounds, indeed! Jack had made up his mind to twenty! Twenty solid golden sovereigns!

He was just settling what he should buy his mother as a fairing, out of the money, when he saw a queer little old man on the road who called out, "Good-morning, Jack!"

"Good-morning," replied Jack, with a polite bow, wondering how the queer little old man happened to know his name; though, to be sure, Jacks were as plentiful as blackberries.

"And where may you be going?" asked the queer little old man. Jack wondered again—he was always wondering, you know—what the queer little old man had to do with it; but, being always polite, he replied:

"I am going to market to sell Milky-White—and I mean to make a good bargain."

"So you will! So you will!" chuckled the queer little old man. "You look the sort of chap for it. I bet you know how many beans make five?"

"Two in each hand and one in my mouth," answered Jack readily. He really was sharp as a needle.

"Just so, just so!" chuckled the queer little old man; and as he spoke he drew out of his pocket five beans. "Well, here they are, so give us Milky-White."

Jack was so flabbergasted that he stood with his mouth open as if he expected the fifth bean to fly into it.

"What!" he said at last. "My Milky-White for five common beans! Not if I know it!"

"But they aren't common beans," put in the queer little old man, and there was a queer little smile on his queer little face. "If you plant these beans over-night, by morning they will have grown up right into the very sky."

Jack was too flabbergasted this time even to open his mouth; his eyes opened instead.

"Did you say right into the very sky?" he asked at last; for, see you, Jack had wondered more about the sky than about anything else.

"*Right up into the very sky*," repeated the queer old man, with a nod between each word. "It's a good bargain, Jack; and, as fair play's a jewel, if they don't—why! meet me here to-morrow morning and you shall have Milky-White back again. Will that please you?"

"Right as a trivet," cried Jack, without stopping to think, and the next moment he found himself standing on an empty road.

"Two in each hand and one in my mouth," repeated Jack. "That is what I said, and what I'll do. Everything in order, and if what the queer little old man said isn't true, I shall get Milky-White back to-morrow morning."

So whistling and munching the bean he trudged home cheerfully, wondering what the sky would be like if he ever got there.

"What a long time you've been!" exclaimed his mother, who was watching anxiously for him at the gate. "It is past sun-setting; but I see you have sold Milky-White. Tell me quick how much you got for her."

125

"You'll never guess," began Jack.

"Laws-a-mercy! You don't say so," interrupted the good woman. "And I worrying all day lest they should take you in. What was it? Ten pounds—fifteen—sure it *can't* be twenty!"

Jack held out the beans triumphantly.

"There," he said. "That's what I got for her, and a jolly good bargain too!"

It was his mother's turn to be flabbergasted; but all she said was:

"What! Them beans!"

"Yes," replied Jack, beginning to doubt his own wisdom; "but they're *magic* beans. If you plant them over-night, by morning they—grow—right up—into—the—sky—Oh! Please don't hit so hard!"

For Jack's mother for once had lost her temper, and was belabouring the boy for all she was worth. And when she had finished scolding and beating, she flung the miserable beans out of the window, and sent him, supperless, to bed.

If this was the magical effect of the beans, thought Jack ruefully, he didn't want any more magic, if you please.

However, being healthy and, as a rule, happy, he soon fell asleep and slept like a top.

When he woke he thought at first it was moonlight, for everything in the room showed greenish. Then he stared at the little window. It was covered as if with a curtain by leaves. He was out of bed in a trice, and the next moment, without waiting to dress, was climbing up the biggest beanstalk you ever saw. For what the queer little old man had said was true! One of the beans which his mother had chucked into the garden had found soil, taken root, and grown in the night . . . .

Where? . . . .

Up to the very sky? Jack meant to see at any rate.

So he climbed, and he climbed, and he climbed. It was easy work, for the big beanstalk with the leaves growing out of each side was like a ladder; for all that he soon was out of breath. Then he got his second wind, and was just beginning to wonder if he had a third when he saw in front of him a wide, shining white road stretching away, and away, and away.

So he took to walking, and he walked, and walked, and walked, till he came to a tall, shining white house with a wide white doorstep.

And on the doorstep stood a great big woman with a black porridge-pot in her hand. Now Jack, having had no supper, was hungry as a hunter, and when he saw the porridge-pot he said quite politely:

"Good-morning, 'm. I wonder if you *could* give me some breakfast?"

"Breakfast!" echoed the woman, who, in truth, was an ogre's wife. "If it is breakfast you're wanting, it's breakfast you'll likely be; for I expect my man home every instant, and there is nothing he likes better for breakfast than a boy—a fat boy grilled on toast."

Now Jack was not a bit of a coward, and when he wanted a thing he generally got it, so he said cheerful-like:

"I'd be fatter if I'd had my breakfast!" Whereat the ogre's wife laughed and bade Jack come in; for she was not, really, half as bad as she looked. But he had hardly finished the great bowl of porridge and milk she gave him when the whole house began to tremble and quake. It was the ogre coming home!

Thump! THUMP! THUMP!!!

"Into the oven with you, sharp!" cried the ogre's wife; and the iron oven door was just closed when the ogre strode in. Jack could see him through the little peep-hole slide at the top where the steam came out.

He was a big one for sure. He had three sheep strung to his belt, and these he threw down on the table. "Here, wife," he cried, "roast me these snippets for breakfast; they are all I've been able to get this morning, worse luck! I hope the oven's hot?" And he went to touch the handle, while Jack burst out all of a sweat, wondering what would happen next.

"Roast!" echoed the ogre's wife. "Pooh! the little things would dry to cinders. Better boil them."

So she set to work to boil them; but the ogre began sniffing about the room. "They don't smell—mutton meat," he growled. Then he frowned horribly and began the real ogre's rhyme:

> "Fee-fi-fo-fum,
> I smell the blood of an Englishman.
> Be he alive, or be he dead,
> I'll grind his bones to make my bread."

"Don't be silly!" said his wife. "It's the bones of the little boy you had for supper that I'm boiling down for soup! Come, eat your breakfast, there's a good ogre!"

So the ogre ate his three sheep, and when he had done he went to a big oaken chest and took out three big bags of golden pieces. These he put on the table, and began to count their contents while his wife cleared away the breakfast things. And by and by his head began to nod, and at last he began to snore, and snored so loud that the whole house shook.

Then Jack slipped out of the oven and, seizing one of the bags of gold, crept away, and ran along the straight, wide, shining white road as fast as his legs would carry him till he came to the beanstalk. He couldn't climb down it with the bag of gold, it was so heavy, so he just flung his burden down first, and, helter-skelter, climbed after it.

And when he came to the bottom, there was his mother picking up gold pieces out of the garden as fast as she could; for, of course, the bag had burst.

"Laws-a-mercy me!" she says. "Wherever have you been? See! It's been rainin' gold!"

"No, it hasn't," began Jack. "I climbed up—" Then he turned to look for the beanstalk; but, lo and behold! it wasn't there at all! So he knew, then, it was all real magic.

After that they lived happily on the gold pieces for a long time, and the bedridden father got all sorts of nice things to eat; but, at last, a day came when Jack's mother showed a doleful face as she put a big yellow sovereign into Jack's hand and bade him be careful marketing, because there was not one more in the coffer. After that they must starve.

That night Jack went supperless to bed of his own accord. If he couldn't make money, he thought, at any rate he could eat less money. It was a shame for a big boy to stuff himself and bring no grist to the mill.

He slept like a top, as boys do when they don't overeat themselves, and when he woke . . .

Hey, presto! the whole room showed greenish, and there was a curtain of leaves over the window! Another bean had grown in the night, and Jack was up it like a lamp-lighter before you could say knife.

This time he didn't take nearly so long climbing until he reached the straight, wide, white road, and in a trice he found himself before the tall white house, where on the wide white steps the ogre's wife was standing with the black porridge-pot in her hand.

And this time Jack was as bold as brass. "Good-morning, 'm," he said. "I've come to ask you for breakfast, for I had no supper, and I'm as hungry as a hunter."

"Fee-fi-fo-fum, I smell the blood of an Englishman."

"Fee-fi-fo-fum, I smell the blood of an Englishman."

"Go away, bad boy!" replied the ogre's wife. "Last time I gave a boy breakfast my man missed a whole bag of gold. I believe you are the same boy."

"Maybe I am, maybe I'm not," said Jack, with a laugh. "I'll tell you true when I've had my breakfast; but not till then."

So the ogre's wife, who was dreadfully curious, gave him a big bowl full of porridge; but before he had half finished it he heard the ogre coming——

Thump! THUMP! THUMP!

"In with you to the oven," shrieked the ogre's wife. "You shall tell me when he has gone to sleep."

This time Jack saw through the steam peep-hole that the ogre had three fat calves strung to his belt.

"Better luck to-day, wife!" he cried, and his voice shook the house. "Quick! Roast these trifles for my breakfast! I hope the oven's hot!"

And he went to feel the handle of the door, but his wife cried out sharply:

"Roast! Why, you'd have to wait hours before they were done! I'll broil them—see how bright the fire is!"

"Umph!" growled the ogre. And then he began sniffing and calling out:

"Fee-fi-fo-fum,
I smell the blood of an Englishman.
Be he alive, or be he dead,
I'll grind his bones to make my bread."

"Twaddle!" said the ogre's wife. "It's only the bones of the boy you had last week that I've put into the pig-bucket!"

"Umph! said the ogre harshly; but he ate the broiled calves, and then he said to his wife, "Bring me my hen that lays the magic eggs. I want to see gold."

So the ogre's wife brought him a great big black hen with a shiny red comb. She plumped it down on the table and took away the breakfast things.

Then the ogre said to the hen, "Lay!" and it promptly laid—what do you think?—a beautiful, shiny, yellow, golden egg!

"None so dusty, henny-penny," laughed the ogre. "I shan't have to beg as long as I've got you." Then he said, "Lay!" once more; and, lo and behold!

131

there was another beautiful, shiny, yellow, golden egg!

Jack could hardly believe his eyes, and made up his mind that he would have that hen, come what might. So, when the ogre began to doze, he just out like a flash from the oven, seized the hen, and ran for his life! But, you see, he reckoned without his prize; for hens, you know, always cackle when they leave their nests after laying an egg, and this one set up such a scrawing that it woke the ogre.

"Where's my hen?" he shouted, and his wife came rushing in, and they both rushed to the door; but Jack had got the better of them by a good start, and all they could see was a little figure right away down the wide white road, holding a big, scrawing, cackling, fluttering black hen by the legs!

How Jack got down the beanstalk he never knew. It was all wings, and leaves, and feathers, and cacklings; but get down he did, and there was his mother wondering if the sky was going to fall!

But the very moment Jack touched ground he called out, "Lay!" and the black hen ceased cackling and laid a great, big, shiny, yellow, golden egg.

So every one was satisfied; and from that moment everybody had everything that money could buy. For, whenever they wanted anything, they just said, "Lay!" and the black hen provided them with gold.

But Jack began to wonder if he couldn't find something else besides money in the sky. So one fine moonlight midsummer night he refused his supper, and before he went to bed stole out to the garden with a big watering-can and watered the ground under his window; for, thought he, "there must be two more beans somewhere, and perhaps it is too dry for them to grow." Then he slept like a top.

And, lo and behold! when he woke, there was the green light shimmering through his room, and there he was in an instant on the beanstalk, climbing, climbing, climbing for all he was worth.

But this time he knew better than to ask for breakfast; for the ogre's wife would be sure to recognize him. So he just hid in some bushes beside the great white house, till he saw her in the scullery, and then he slipped out and hid himself in the copper; for he knew she would be sure to look in the oven first thing.

And by and by he heard—

Thump! THUMP! THUMP!

And peeping through a crack in the copper-lid, he could see the ogre stalk in with three huge oxen strung at his belt. But this time, no sooner had the ogre got into the house than he began shouting:

"Fee-fi-fo-fum,
I smell the blood of an Englishman.
Be he alive, or be he dead,
I'll grind his bones to make my bread."

For, see you, the copper-lid didn't fit tight like the oven door, and ogres have noses like a dog's for scent.

"Well, I declare, so do I!" exclaimed the ogre's wife. "It will be that horrid boy who stole the bag of gold and the hen. If so, he's hid in the oven!"

But when she opened the door, lo and behold! Jack wasn't there! Only some joints of meat roasting and sizzling away. Then she laughed and said, "You and me be fools for sure. Why, it's the boy you caught last night as I was getting ready for your breakfast. Yes, we be fools to take dead meat for live flesh! So eat your breakfast, there's a good ogre!"

But the ogre, though he enjoyed roast boy very much, wasn't satisfied, and every now and then he would burst out with *"Fee-fi-fo-fum,"* and get up and search the cupboards, keeping Jack in a fever of fear lest he should think of the copper.

But he didn't. And when he had finished his breakfast he called out to his wife, "Bring me my magic harp! I want to be amused."

So she brought out a little harp and put it on the table. And the ogre leant back in his chair and said lazily:

"Sing!"

And, lo and behold! the harp began to sing. If you want to know what it sang about? Why! It sang about everything! And it sang so beautifully that Jack forgot to be frightened, and the ogre forgot to think of *"Fee-fi-fo-fum,"* and fell asleep and

did — n o t — s n o r e.

Then Jack stole out of the copper like a mouse and crept hands and knees to the table, raised himself up ever so softly and laid hold of the magic harp; for he was determined to have it.

But, no sooner had he touched it, than it cried out quite loud, "Master! Master!" So the ogre woke, saw Jack making off, and rushed after him.

My goodness, it was a race! Jack was nimble, but the ogre's stride was twice as long. So, though Jack turned, and twisted, and doubled like a hare, yet at last, when he got to the beanstalk, the ogre was not a dozen yards behind him. There wasn't time to think, so Jack just flung himself on to the stalk and began to go down as fast as he could, while the harp kept calling, "Master! Master!" at the very top of its voice. He had only got down about a quarter of the way when there was the most awful lurch you can think of, and Jack nearly fell off the beanstalk. It was the ogre beginning to climb down, and his weight made the stalk sway like a tree in a storm. Then Jack knew it was life or death, and he climbed down faster and faster, and as he climbed he shouted, "Mother! Mother! Bring an axe! Bring an axe!"

Now his mother, as luck would have it, was in the back-yard chopping wood, and she ran out thinking that this time the sky must have fallen. Just at that moment Jack touched the ground, and he flung down the harp — which immediately began to sing of all sorts of beautiful things — and he seized the axe and gave a great chop at the beanstalk, which shook and swayed and bent like barley before a breeze.

"Have a care!" shouted the ogre, clinging on as hard as he could. But Jack *did* have a care, and he dealt that beanstalk such a shrewd blow that the whole of it, ogre and all, came toppling down, and, of course, the ogre broke his crown, so that he died on the spot.

After that every one was quite happy. For they had gold and to spare, and if the bedridden father was dull, Jack just brought out the harp and said, "Sing!" And, lo and behold! it sang about every-thing under the sun.

JACK AND THE BEANSTALK

So Jack ceased wondering so much and became quite a useful person.
And the last bean hasn't grown yet. It is still in the garden.
I wonder if it will every grow?
And what little child will climb its beanstalk into the sky?
And what will that child find?
Goody me!

THE FISH
AND THE RING

THE FISH
AND THE RING

Once upon a time there lived a Baron who was a great magician, and could tell by his arts and charms everything that was going to happen at any time.

Now this great lord had a little son born to him.as heir to all his castles and lands. So, when the little lad was about four years old, wishing to know what his fortune would be, the Baron looked in his Book of Fate to see what it foretold.

And, lo and behold! it was written that this much-loved, much-prized heir to all the great lands and castles was to marry a low-born maiden. So the Baron was dismayed, and set to work by more arts and charms to discover if this maiden were already born, and if so, where she lived.

And he found out that she had just been born in a very poor house, where the poor parents were already burdened with five children.

So he called for his horse and rode away, and away, until he came to the poor man's house, and there he found the poor man sitting at his doorstep very sad and doleful.

"What is the matter, my friend?" asked he; and the poor man replied:

"May it please your honour, a little lass has just been born to our house; and we have five children already, and where the bread is to come from to fill the sixth mouth, we know not."

"If that be all your trouble," quoth the Baron readily, "mayhap I can help you: so don't be down-hearted. I am just looking for such a little lass to companion my son, so, if you will, I will give you ten crowns for her."

Well! the man he nigh jumped for joy, since he was to get good money, and his daughter, so he thought, a good home. Therefore he brought out the child then and there, and the Baron, wrapping the babe in his cloak, rode away. But when he got to the river he flung the little thing into the swollen stream, and said to himself as he galloped back to his castle:

"There goes Fate!"

But, you see, he was just sore mistaken. For the little lass didn't sink. The stream was very swift, and her long clothes kept her up till she caught in a snag just opposite a fisherman, who was mending his nets.

Now the fisherman and his wife had no children, and they were just longing for a baby; so when the goodman saw the little lass he was overcome with joy, and took her home to his wife, who received her with open arms.

And there she grew up, the apple of their eyes, into the most beautiful maiden that ever was seen.

Now, when she was about fifteen years of age, it so happened that the Baron and his friends went a-hunting along the banks of the river and stopped to get a drink of water at the fisherman's hut. And who should bring the water out but, as they thought, the fisherman's daughter.

Now the young men of the party noticed her beauty, and one of them said to the Baron, "She should marry well; read us her fate, since you are so learned in the art."

Then the Baron, scarce looking at her, said carelessly: "I could guess her fate! Some wretched yokel or other. But, to please you, I will cast her horoscope by the stars; so tell me, girl, what day you were born?"

"That I cannot tell, sir," replied the girl, "for I was picked up in the river about fifteen years ago."

Then the Baron grew pale, for he guessed at once that she was the little lass he had flung into the stream, and that Fate had been stronger than he was. But he kept his own counsel and said nothing at the time. Afterwards, however, he thought out a plan, so he rode back and gave the girl a letter.

"See you!" he said. "I will make your fortune. Take this letter to my brother, who needs a good girl, and you will be settled for life."

Now the fisherman and his wife were growing old and needed help; so the girl said she would go, and took the letter.

And the Baron rode back to his castle saying to himself once more:

"There goes Fate!"

For what he had written in the letter was this:

"Dear Brother,
    Take the bearer and put her to death immediately."

The fisherman and his wife had no children,
and they were just longing for a baby.

But once again he was sore mistaken; since on the way to the town where his brother lived, the girl had to stop the night in a little inn. And it so happened that that very night a gang of thieves broke into the inn, and not content with carrying off all that the innkeeper possessed, they searched the pockets of the guests, and found the letter which the girl carried. And when they read it, they agreed that it was a mean trick and a shame. So their captain sat down and, taking pen and paper, wrote instead:

"Dear Brother,
   Take the bearer and marry her to my son without delay."

Then, after putting the note into an envelope and sealing it up, they gave it to the girl and bade her go on her way. So when she arrived at the brother's castle, though rather surprised, he gave orders for a wedding feast to be prepared. And the Baron's son, who was staying with his uncle, seeing the girl's great beauty, was nothing loth, so they were fast wedded.

Well! when the news was brought to the Baron, he was nigh beside himself; but he was determined not to be done by Fate. So he rode post-haste to his brother's and pretended to be quite pleased. And then one day, when no one was nigh, he asked the young bride to come for a walk with him, and when they were close to some cliffs, seized hold of her, and was for throwing her over into the sea. But she begged hard for her life.

"It is not my fault," she said. "I have done nothing. It is Fate. But if you will spare my life I promise that I will fight against Fate also. I will never see you or your son again until you desire it. That will be safer for you; since, see you, the sea may preserve me, as the river did."

Well! The Baron agreed to this. So he took off his gold ring from his finger and flung it over the cliffs into the sea and said:

"Never dare to show me your face again till you can show me that ring likewise."

And with that he let her go.

Well! the girl wandered on, and she wandered on, until she came to a nobleman's castle; and there, as they needed a kitchen girl, she engaged as a scullion, since she had been used to such work in the fisherman's hut.

Now one day, as she was cleaning a big fish, she looked out of the kitchen window, and who should she see driving up to dinner but the Baron and his young son, her husband. At first she thought that, to keep her promise, she must run away; but afterwards she remembered they would not see her in the kitchen, so she went on with her cleaning of the big fish.

And, lo and behold! she saw something shine in its inside, and there, sure enough, was the Baron's ring! She was glad enough to see it, I can tell you; so she slipped it on to her thumb. But she went on with her work, and dressed the fish as nicely as ever she could, and served it up as pretty as may be, with parsley sauce and butter.

Well! when it came to table the guests liked it so well that they asked the host who cooked it. And he called to his servants, "Send up the cook who cooked that fine fish, that she may get her reward."

Well! when the girl heard she was wanted she made herself ready, and with the gold ring on her thumb, went boldly into the dining-hall. And all the guests when they saw her were struck dumb by her wonderful beauty. And the young husband started up gladly; but the Baron, recognizing her, jumped up angrily and looked as if he would kill her. So, without one word, the girl held up her hand before his face, and the gold ring shone and glittered on it; and she went straight up to the Baron, and laid her hand with the ring on it before him on the table.

Then the Baron understood that Fate had been too strong for him; so he took her by the hand, and, placing her beside him, turned to the guests and said:

"This is my son's wife. Let us drink a toast in her honour."

And after dinner he took her and his son home to his castle, where they all lived as happy as could be for ever afterwards.

THE BOGEY-BEAST

THE BOGEY-BEAST

There was once a woman who was very, very cheerful, though she had little to make her so; for she was old, and poor, and lonely. She lived in a little bit of a cottage and earned a scant living by running errands for her neighbours, getting a bite here, a sup there, as reward for her services. So she made shift to get on, and always looked as spry and cheery as if she had not a want in the world.

Now one summer evening, as she was trotting, full of smiles as ever, along the high road to her hovel, what should she see but a big black pot lying in the ditch!

"Goodness me!" she cried, "that would be just the very thing for me if I only had something to put in it! But I haven't! Now who could have left it in the ditch?"

And she looked about her expecting the owner would not be far off; but she could see nobody.

"Maybe there is a hole in it," she went on, "and that's why it has been cast away. But it would do fine to put a flower in for my window; so I'll just take it home with me."

And with that she lifted the lid and looked inside.

"Mercy me!" she cried, fair amazed. "If it isn't full of gold pieces. Here's luck!"

And so it was, brimful of great gold coins. Well, at first she simply stood stock-still, wondering if she was standing on her head or her heels. Then she began saying:

"Lawks! But I *do* feel rich!"

After she had said this many times, she began to wonder how she was to get her treasure home. It was too heavy for her to carry, and she could see no better way than to tie the end of her shawl to it and drag it behind her like a go-cart.

"It will soon be dark," she said to herself as she trotted along. "So much the better! The neighbours will not see what I'm bringing home, and I shall have all the night to myself, and be able to think what I'll do! Mayhap I'll buy a grand house and just sit by the fire with a cup o' tea and do no work at all like a queen. Or maybe I'll bury it at the garden foot and just keep a bit in the old china teapot on the chimney-piece. Or maybe— Goody! Goody! I feel that grand I don't know myself."

By this time she was a bit tired of dragging such a heavy weight, and, stopping to rest a while, turned to look at her treasure.

And lo! it wasn't a pot of gold at all! It was nothing but a lump of silver.

She stared at it, and rubbed her eyes, and stared at it again.

"Well! I never!" she said at last. "And me thinking it was a pot of gold! I must have been dreaming. But this is luck! Silver is far less trouble—easier to mind, and not so easy stolen. Them gold pieces would have been the death o' me, and with this great lump of silver—"

So she went off again planning what she would do, and feeling as rich as rich, until becoming a bit tired again she stopped to rest and gave a look round to see if her treasure was safe; and she saw nothing but a great lump of iron!

"Well! I never!" says she again. "And I mistaking it for silver! I must have been dreaming. But this is luck! It's real convenient. I can get penny pieces for old iron, and penny pieces are a deal handier for me than your gold and silver. Why! I should never have slept a wink for fear of being robbed. But a penny piece comes in useful, and I shall sell that iron for a lot and be real rich—rolling rich."

So on she trotted full of plans as to how she would spend her penny pieces, till once more she stopped to rest and looked round to see her treasure was safe. And this time she saw nothing but a big stone.

"Well! I never!" she cried, full of smiles. "And to think I mistook it for iron. I must have been dreaming. But here's luck indeed, and me wanting a stone terrible bad to stick open the gate. Eh my! but it's a change for the better! It's a fine thing to have good luck."

So, all in a hurry to see how the stone would keep the gate open, she trotted off down the hill till she came to her own cottage. She unlatched the gate and then turned to unfasten her shawl from the stone which lay on the path behind her. Aye! It was a stone sure enough. There was plenty light to see it

"Well!" she chuckled, "I am in luck!"

lying there, douce and peaceable as a stone should.

So she bent over it to unfasten the shawl end, when——

"Oh my!"

All of a sudden it gave a jump, a squeal, and in one moment was as big as a haystack. Then it let down four great lanky legs and threw out two long ears, flourished a great long tail and romped off, kicking and squealing and shinnying and laughing like a naughty, mischievous boy!

The old woman stared after it till it was fairly out of sight, then she burst out laughing too.

"Well!" she chuckled, "I am in luck! Quite the luckiest body hereabouts. Fancy my seeing the Bogey-Beast all to myself; and making myself so free with it too! My goodness! I do feel that uplifted—that *GRAND!*"——

So she went into her cottage and spent the evening chuckling over her good luck.

THE TWO SISTERS

THE TWO SISTERS

Once upon a time there were two sisters who were as like each other as two peas in a pod; but one was good, and the other was bad-tempered. Now their father had no work, so the girls began to think of going to service.

"I will go first and see what I can make of it," said the younger sister, ever so cheerfully, "then you, sis, can follow if I have good luck."

So she packed up a bundle, said good-bye, and started to find a place; but no one in the town wanted a girl, and she went farther afield into the country. And as she journeyed she came upon an oven in which a lot of loaves were baking. Now as she passed, the loaves cried out with one voice:

"Little girl! Little girl! Take us out! Please take us out! We have been baking for seven years, and no one has come to take us out. Do take us out or we shall soon be burnt!"

Then, being a kind, obliging little girl, she stopped, put down her bundle, took out the bread, and went on her way saying:

"You will be more comfortable now."

After a time she came to a cow lowing beside an empty pail, and the cow said to her:

"Little girl! Little girl! Milk me! Please milk me! Seven years have I been waiting, but no one has come to milk me!"

So the kind girl stopped, put down her bundle, milked the cow into the pail, and went on her way saying:

"Now you will be more comfortable."

By and by she came to an apple tree so laden with fruit that its branches were nigh to break, and the apple tree called to her:

"Little girl! Little girl! Please shake my branches. The fruit is so heavy I can't stand straight!"

Then the kind girl stopped, put down her bundle, and shook the branches so that the apples fell off, and the tree could stand straight. Then she went on her way saying:

"You will be more comfortable now."

So she journeyed on till she came to a house where an old witch-woman lived. Now this witch-woman wanted a servant-maid, and promised good wages. Therefore the girl agreed to stop with her and try how she liked service. She had to sweep the floor, keep the house clean and tidy, the fire bright and cheery. But there was one thing the witch-woman said she must never do; and that was look up the chimney!

"If you do," said the witch-woman, "something will fall down on you, and you will come to a bad end."

"Well! the girl swept, and dusted, and made up the fire; but ne'er a penny of wages did she see. Now the girl wanted to go home as she did not like witch-service; for the witch used to have boiled babies for supper, and bury the bones under some stones in the garden. But she did not like to go home penniless; so she stayed on, sweeping, and dusting, and doing her work, just as if she was pleased. Then one day, as she was sweeping up the hearth, down tumbled some soot, and, without remembering she was forbidden to look up the chimney, she looked up to see where the soot came from. And, lo and behold! a big bag of gold fell plump into her lap.

Now the witch happened to be out on one of her witch errands; so the girl thought it a fine opportunity to be off home.

So she kilted up her petticoats and started to run home; but she had only gone a little way when she heard the witch-woman coming after her on her broomstick. Now the apple tree she had helped to stand straight happened to be quite close; so she ran to it and cried:

"Apple tree! Apple tree, hide me
So the old witch can't find me,
For if she does she'll pick my bones,
And bury me under the garden stones."

Then the apple tree said, "Of course I will. You helped me to stand straight, and one good turn deserves another."

"Tree of mine! O Tree of mine!
Have you seen my naughty little maid?"

So the apple tree hid her finely in its green branches; and when the witch flew past saying:

> 'Tree of mine! O Tree of mine!
> Have you seen my naughty little maid
> With a willy willy wag and a great big bag?
> She's stolen my money—all I had!"

The apple tree answered:

> 'No, mother dear,
> Not for seven year!"

So the witch flew on the wrong way, and the girl got down, thanked the tree politely, and started again. But just as she got to where the cow was standing beside the pail, she heard the witch coming again, so she ran to the cow and cried:

> "Cow! Cow, please hide me
> So the witch can't find me;
> If she does she'll pick my bones,
> And bury me under the garden stones!"

"Certainly I will," answered the cow. "Didn't you milk me and make me comfortable? Hide yourself behind me and you'll be quite safe."
And when the witch flew by and called to the cow:

> "O Cow of mine! Cow of mine!
> Have you seen my naughty little maid
> With a willy willy wag and a great big bag,
> Who stole my money—all that I had?"

she just said politely:

> 'No, mother dear,
> Not for seven year!"

Then the old witch went on in the wrong direction, and the girl started afresh on her way home; but just as she got to where the oven stood, she heard that horrid old witch coming behind her again; so she ran as fast as she could to the oven and cried:

> "O Oven! Oven! hide me
> So as the witch can't find me,
> For if she does she'll pick my bones,
> And bury them under the garden stones."

Then the oven said, "I am afraid there is no room for you, as another batch of bread is baking; but there is the baker—ask him."

So she asked the baker, and he said, "Of course I will. You saved my last batch from being burnt; so run into the bakehouse, you will be quite safe there, and I will settle the witch for you."

So she hid in the bakehouse, only just in time, for there was the old witch calling angrily:

> "O Man of mine! Man of mine!
> Have you seen my naughty little maid
> With a willy willy wag and a great big bag,
> Who's stole my money—all I had?"

Then the baker replied, "Look in the oven. She may be there."

And the witch alighted from her broomstick and peered into the oven: but she could see no one.

"Creep in and look in the farthest corner," said the baker slyly, and the witch crept in, when—

Bang!—

he shut the door in her face, and there she was roasting. And when she came out with the bread she was all crisp and brown, and had to go home as best she could and put cold cream all over her!

But the kind, obliging little girl got safe home with her bag of money.

THE TWO SISTERS

Now the ill-tempered elder sister was very jealous of this good luck, and determined to get a bag of gold for herself. So she in her turn packed up a bundle and started to seek service by the same road. But when she came to the oven, and the loaves begged her to take them out because they had been baking seven years and were nigh to burning, she tossed her head and said:

"A likely story indeed, that I should burn my fingers to save your crusts. No, thank you!"

And with that she went on till she came across the cow standing waiting to be milked beside the pail. But when the cow said:

"Little girl! Little girl! Milk me! Please milk me, I've waited seven years to be milked—"

She only laughed and replied, "You may wait another seven years for all I care. I'm not your dairymaid!"

And with that she went on till she came to the apple tree, all overburdened by its fruit. But when it begged her to shake its branches, she only giggled, and plucking one ripe apple, said:

"One is enough for me: you can keep the rest yourself."

And with that she went on munching the apple, till she came to the witch-woman's house.

Now the witch-woman, though she had got over being crisp and brown from the oven, was dreadfully angry with all little maid-servants, and made up her mind this one should not trick her. So for a long time she never went out of the house; thus the ill-tempered sister never had a chance of looking up the chimney, as she had meant to do at once. And she had to dust, and clean, and brush, and sweep ever so hard, until she was quite tired out.

But one day, when the witch-woman went into the garden to bury her bones, she seized the moment, looked up the chimney, and, sure enough, a bag of gold fell plump into her lap!

Well! she was off with it in a moment, and ran and ran till she came to the apple tree, when she heard the witch-woman behind her. So she cried as her sister had done:

"Apple tree! Apple tree, hide me
So the old witch can't find me,
For if she does she'll break my bones
Or bury me under the garden stones."

But the apple tree said:

"No room here! I've too many apples."

So she had to run on; and when the witch-woman on her broomstick came flying by and called:

> "O Tree of mine! Tree of mine!
> Have you seen a naughty little maid
> With a willy willy wag and a great big bag,
> Who's stolen my money—all I had?"

the apple tree replied:

> "Yes, mother dear,
> She's gone down there."

Then the witch-woman went after her, caught her, gave her a thorough good beating, took the bag of money away from her, and sent her home without a penny payment for all her dusting, and sweeping, and brushing, and cleaning.

THE GOLDEN SNUFF-BOX

THE GOLDEN SNUFF-BOX

Once upon a time, and a very good time too, though it was not in my time, nor your time, nor for the matter of that in any one's time, there lived a man and a woman who had one son called Jack, and he was just terribly fond of reading books. He read, and he read, and then, because his parents lived in a lonely house in a lonely forest and he never saw any other folk but his father and his mother, he became quite crazy to go out into the world and see charming princesses and the like.

So one day he told his mother he must be off, and she called him an air-brained addle-pate, but added that, as he was no use at home, he had better go seek his fortune. Then she asked him if he would rather take a small cake with her blessing to eat on his journey, or a large cake with her curse? Now Jack was a very hungry lad, so he just up and said:

"A big cake, if you plase, 'm."

So his mother made a great big cake, and when he started she just off to the top of the house and cast malisons on him, till he got out of sight. You see she had to do it, but after that she sate down and cried.

Well, Jack hadn't gone far till he came to a field where his father was ploughing. Now the goodman was dreadfully put out when he found his son was going away, and still more so when he heard he had chosen his mother's malison. So he cast about what to do to put things straight, and at last he drew out of his pocket a little golden snuff-box, and gave it to the lad, saying:

"If ever you are in danger of sudden death you may open the box; but not till then. It has been in our family for years and years; but, as we have lived, father and son, quietly in the forest, none of us have ever been in need of help—perhaps you may."

So Jack pocketed the golden snuff-box and went on his way.

Now, after a time, he grew very tired, and very hungry, for he had eaten his big cake first thing, and night closed in on him so that he could scarce see his way.

But at last he came to a large house and begged board and lodging at the back door. Now Jack was a good-looking young fellow, so the maid-servant at once called him in to the fireside and gave him plenty good meat and bread and beer. And it so happened that while he was eating his supper the master's gay young daughter came into the kitchen and saw him. So she went to her father and said that there was the prettiest young fellow she had ever seen in the back kitchen, and that if her father loved her he would give the young man some employment. Now the gentleman of the house was exceedingly fond of his gay young daughter, and did not want to vex her; so he went into the back kitchen and questioned Jack as to what he could do.

"Anything," said Jack gaily, meaning, of course, that he could do any foolish bit of work about a house.

But the gentleman saw a way of pleasing his gay young daughter and getting rid of the trouble of employing Jack; so he laughs and says, "If you can do anything, my good lad," says he, "you had better do this. By eight o'clock to-morrow morning you must have dug a lake four miles round in front of my mansion, and on it there must be floating a whole fleet of vessels. And they must range up in front of my mansion and fire a salute of guns. And the very last shot must break the leg of the four-post bed on which my daughter sleeps, for she is always late of a morning!"

Well! Jack was terribly flabbergasted, but he faltered out:

"And if I don't do it?"

"Then," said the master of the house quite calmly, "your life will be the forfeit."

So he bade the servants take Jack to a turret-room and lock the door on him.

Well! Jack sate on the side of his bed and tried to think things out, but he felt as if he didn't know *b* from a battledore, so he decided to think no more, and after saying his prayers he lay down and went to sleep. And he did sleep! When he woke it was close on eight o'clock, and he had only time to fly to the window and look out, when the great clock on the tower began to whirr before it struck the hour. And there was the lawn in front of the house all set with beds of roses and stocks and marigolds! Well! all of a sudden he remembered the little golden snuff-box.

"I'm near enough to death," quoth he to himself, as he drew it out and opened it.

And no sooner had he opened it than out hopped three funny little red men in red nightcaps, rubbing their eyes and yawning; for, see you, they had been locked up in the box for years, and years, and years.

"What do you want, Master?" they said between their yawns. But Jack heard that clock a-whirring and knew he hadn't a moment to lose, so he just grabbled off his orders. Then the clock began to strike, and the little men flew out of the window, and suddenly

Bang! bang! bang! bang! bang! bang!

went the guns, and the last one must have broken the leg of the four-post bed, for there at the window was the gay young daughter in her nightcap, gazing with astonishment at the lake four miles round, with the fleet of vessels floating on it!

And so did Jack! He had never seen such a sight in his life, and he was quite sorry when the three little red men disturbed him by flying in at the window and scrambling into the golden snuff-box.

"Give us a little more time when you want us next, Master," they said sulkily. Then they shut down the lid, and Jack could hear them yawning inside as they settled down to sleep.

As you may imagine, the master of the house was fair astonished, while as for the gay young daughter, she declared at once that she would never marry any one else but the young man who could do such wonderful things; the truth being that she and Jack had fallen in love with each other at first sight.

But her father was cautious. "It is true, my dear," says he, "that the young fellow seems a bully boy; but for aught we know it may be chance, not skill, and he may have a broken feather in his wing. So we must try him again."

Then he said to Jack, "My daughter must have a fine house to live in. Therefore by to-morrow morning at eight o'clock there must be a magnificent castle standing on twelve golden pillars in the middle of the lake, and there must be a church beside it. And all things must be ready for the bride, and at eight o'clock precisely a peal of bells from the church must ring out for the wedding. If not you will have to forfeit your life."

This time Jack intended to give the three little red men more time for their task; but what with having enjoyed himself so much all day, and having eaten so much good food, he overslept himself, so that the big clock on the tower was whirring before it struck eight when he woke, leapt out of bed, and rushed to the golden snuff-box. But he had forgotten where he had put it, and so the clock had *really* begun to strike before he found it under his pillow, opened it, and gabbled out his orders. And then you never saw how the three little red men tumbled over each other and yawned and stretched and made haste all at one time, so that Jack thought his life would surely be forfeit. But just as the clock struck its last chime, out rang a peal of merry bells, and there was the Castle standing on twelve golden pillars and a church beside it in the middle of the lake. And the Castle was all decorated for the wedding, and there were crowds and crowds of servants and retainers, all dressed in their Sunday best.

Never had Jack seen such a sight before; neither had the gay young daughter who, of course, was looking out of the next window in her nightcap. And she looked so pretty and so gay that Jack felt quite cross when he had to step back to let the three little red men fly to their golden snuff-box. But they were far crosser than he was, and mumbled and grumbled at the hustle, so that Jack was quite glad when they shut the box down and began to snore.

Well, of course, Jack and the gay young daughter were married, and were as happy as the day is long; and Jack had fine clothes to wear, fine food to eat, fine servants to wait on him, and as may fine friends as he liked.

So he was in luck; but he had yet to learn that a mother's malison is sure to bring misfortune some time or another.

Thus it happened that one day when he was going a-hunting with all the ladies and gentlemen, Jack forgot to change the golden snuff-box (which he always carried about with him for fear of accidents) from his waistcoat pocket to that of his scarlet hunting-coat; so he left it behind him. And what should happen but that the servant let it fall on the ground when he was folding up the clothes, and the snuff-box flew open and out popped the three little red men yawning and stretching.

Well! when they found out that they hadn't really been summoned, and that there was no fear of death, they were in a towering temper and said they had a great mind to fly away with the Castle, golden pillars and all.

On hearing this the servant pricked up his ears.

"Could you do that?" he asked.

"Could we?" they said, and they laughed loud. "Why, we can do anything."

Then the servant said ever so sharp, "Then move me this Castle and all it contains right away over the sea where the master can't disturb us."

Now the little red men need not really have obeyed the order, but they were so cross with Jack that hardly had the servant said the words before the task was done; so when the hunting-party came back, lo and behold! the Castle, and the church, and the golden pillars had all disappeared!

At first all the rest set upon Jack for being a knave and a cheat; and, in particular, his wife's father threatened to have at him for deceiving the gay young daughter; but at last he agreed to let Jack have twelve months and a day to find the Castle and bring it back.

So off Jack starts on a good horse with some money in his pocket.

And he travelled far and he travelled fast, and he travelled east and west, north and south, over hills, and dales, and valleys, and mountains, and woods, and sheepwalks, but never a sign of the missing castle did he see. Now at last he came to the palace of the King of all the Mice and the Wide World. and there was a little mousie in a fine hauberk and a steel cap doing sentry at the front gate, and he was not for letting Jack in until he had told his errand. And when Jack had told it, he passed him on to the next mouse sentry at the inner gate; so by degrees he reached the King's chamber, where he sate surrounded by mice courtiers.

Now the King of the Mice received Jack very graciously, and said that he himself knew nothing of the missing Castle, but, as he was King of all the Mice in the whole world, it was possible that some of his subjects might know more than he. So he ordered his chamberlain to command a Grand Assembly for the next morning, and in the meantime he entertained Jack right royally.

But the next morning, though there were brown mice, and black mice, and grey mice, and white mice, and piebald mice, from all parts of the world, they all answered with one breath:

"If it please your Majesty, we have not seen the missing Castle."

Then the King said, "You must go and ask my elder brother the King of all the Frogs. He may be able to tell you. Leave your horse here and take one of mine. It knows the way and will carry you safe."

So Jack set off on the King's horse, and as he passed the outer gate he saw the little mouse sentry coming away, for its guard was up. Now Jack was a kind-hearted lad, and he had saved some crumbs from his dinner in order to recompense the little sentry for his kindness. So he put his hand in his pocket and pulled out the crumbs.

"Here you are, mousekin," he said. "That's for your trouble!"

Then the mouse thanked him kindly and asked if he would take him along to the King of the Frogs.

"Not I," says Jack. "I should get into trouble with your King."

But the mousekin insisted. "I may be of some use to you," it said. So it ran up the horse's hind leg and up by its tail and hid in Jack's pocket. And the horse set off at a hand gallop, for it didn't half like the mouse running over it.

So at last Jack came to the palace of the King of all the Frogs, and there at the front gate was a frog doing sentry in a fine coat of mail and a brass helmet. And the frog sentry was for not letting Jack in; but the mouse called out that they came from the King of all the Mice and must be let in without delay. So they were taken to the King's chamber, where he sate surrounded by frog courtiers in fine clothes; but alas! he had heard nothing of the Castle on golden pillars, and though he summoned all the frogs of all the world to a Grand Assembly next morning, they all answered his question with:

"Kro kro, Kro kro,"

which every one knows stands for "No" in frog language.

So the King said to Jack, "There remains but one thing. You must go and ask my eldest brother, the King of all the Birds. His subjects are always on the wing, so mayhap they have seen something. Leave the horse you are riding here and take one of mine. It knows the way, and will carry you safe."

So Jack set off, and being a kind-hearted lad he gave the frog sentry, whom he met coming away from his guard, some crumbs he had saved from his dinner. And the frog asked leave to go with him, and when Jack refused to take him he just gave one hop on to the stirrup, and a second hop on to the crupper, and the next hop he was in Jack's other pocket.

Then the horse galloped away like lightning, for it didn't like the slimy frog coming down "plop" on its back.

Well, after a time, Jack came to the palace of the King of all the Birds, and there at the front gate were a sparrow and a crow marching up and down with matchlocks on their shoulders. Now at this Jack laughed fit to split, and the mouse and the frog from his pockets called out:

"We come from the King! Sirrahs! Let us pass."

So that the sentries were right mazed, and let them pass in without more ado.

But when they came to the King's chamber, where he sate surrounded by all manner of birds, tomtits, wrens, cormorants, turtle-doves, and the like, the King said he was sorry, but he had no news of the missing Castle. And though he summoned all the birds of all the world to a Grand Assembly next morning, not one of them had seen or heard tell of it.

So Jack was quite disconsolate till the King said, "But where is the eagle? I don't see my eagle."

Then the Chamberlain—he was a tomtit—stepped forward with a bow and said:

"May it please your Majesty he is late."

"Late?" says the King in a fume. "Summon him at once."

So two larks flew up into the sky till they couldn't be seen and sang ever so loud, till at last the eagle appeared all in a perspiration from having flown so fast.

Then the King said, "Sirrah! Have you seen a missing Castle that stands upon twelve pillars of gold?"

And the eagle blinked its eyes and said, "May it please your Majesty that is where I've been."

Then everybody rejoiced exceedingly, and when the eagle had eaten a whole calf so as to be strong enough for the journey, he spread his wide wings on which Jack stood, with the mouse in one pocket and the frog in the other, and started to obey the King's order to take the owner back to his missing Castle as quickly as possible.

And they flew over land and they flew over sea, until at last in the far distance they saw the Castle standing on its twelve golden pillars. But all the doors and windows were fast shut and barred, for, see you, the servant-master who had run away with it had gone out for the day a-hunting, and he always bolted doors and windows while he was absent lest some one else should run away with it.

Then Jack was puzzled to think how he should get hold of the golden snuff-box, until the little mouse said:

"Let me fetch it. There is always a mouse-hole in every castle, so I am sure I shall be able to get in."

So it went off, and Jack waited on the eagle's wings in a fume; till at last mousekin appeared.

"Have you got it?" shouted Jack, and the little mousie cried:

"Yes!"

So every one rejoiced exceedingly, and they set off back to the palace of the King of all the Birds, where Jack had left his horse; for now that he had the golden snuff-box safe he knew he could get the Castle back whenever he chose to send the three little red men to fetch it. But on the way over the sea, while Jack, who was dead tired with standing so long, lay down between the eagle's wings and fell asleep, the mouse and the eagle fell to quarrelling as to which of them had helped Jack the most, and they quarrelled so much that at last they laid the case before the frog. Then the frog, who made a very wise judge, said he must see the whole affair from the very beginning; so the mouse brought out the golden snuff-box from Jack's pocket, and began to relate where it had been found and all about it. Now, at that very moment Jack awoke, kicked out his leg, and plump went the golden snuff-box down to the very bottom of the sea!

"I thought my turn would come," said the frog, and went plump in after it.

Well, they waited, and waited, and waited for three whole days and three whole nights; but froggie never came up again, and they had just given him up in despair when his nose showed above the water.

"Have you got it?" they shouted.

"No!" says he, with a great gasp.

"Then what do you want?" they cried in a rage.

"My breath," says froggie, and with that he sinks down again.

Well, they waited two days and two nights more, and at last up comes the little frog with the golden snuff-box in its mouth.

Then they all rejoiced exceedingly, and the eagle flew ever so fast to the palace of the King of the Birds.

But alas and alack-a-day! Jack's troubles were not ended; his mother's malison was still bringing him ill-luck, for the King of the Birds flew into a fearsome rage because Jack had not brought the Castle of the golden pillars back with him. And he said that unless he saw it by eight o'clock next morning Jack's head should come off as a cheat and a liar.

Then Jack being close to death opened the golden snuff-box, and out tumbled the three little red men in their little red caps. They had recovered

their tempers and were quite glad to be back with a master who knew that they would only, as a rule, work under fear of death; for, see you, the servant-master had been for ever disturbing their sleep with opening the box to no purpose.

So before the clock struck eight next morning, there was the Castle on its twelve golden pillars, and the King of the Birds was fine and pleased, and let Jack take his horse and ride to the palace of the King of the Frogs. But there exactly the same thing happened, and poor Jack had to open the snuff-box again and order the Castle to come to the palace of the King of the Frogs. At this the little red men were a wee bit cross; but they said they supposed it could not be helped; so, though they yawned, they brought the Castle all right, and Jack was allowed to take his horse and go to the palace of the King of all the Mice in the World. But here the same thing happened, and the little red men tumbled out of the golden snuff-box in a real rage, and said fellows might as well have no sleep at all! However, they did as they were bidden; they brought the Castle of the golden pillars from the palace of the King of the Frogs to the palace of the King of the Birds, and Jack was allowed to take his own horse and ride home.

But the year and a day which he had been allowed was almost gone, and even his gay young wife, after almost weeping her eyes out after her handsome young husband, had given up Jack for lost; so every one was astounded to see him, and not overpleased either to see him come without his Castle. Indeed his father-in-law swore with many oaths that if it were not in its proper place by eight o'clock next morning Jack's life should be forfeit.

Now this, of course, was exactly what Jack had wanted and intended from the beginning; because when death was nigh he could open the golden snuff-box and order about the little red men. But he had opened it so often of late and they had become so cross that he was in a stew what to do; whether to give them time to show their temper, or to hustle them out of it. At last he decided to do half and half. So just as the hands of the clock were at five minutes to eight he opened the box, and stopped his ears!

Well! you never heard such a yawning, and scolding, and threatening, and blustering. What did he mean by it? Why should he take four bites at one cherry? If he was always in fear of death why didn't he die and have done with it?

In the midst of all this the tower clock began to whirr——

"Gentlemen!" says Jack—he was really quaking with fear—"do as you are told."

"For the last time," they shrieked. "We won't stay and serve a master who thinks he is going to die every day."

And with that they flew out of the window.

AND THEY NEVER CAME BACK.

The golden snuff-box remained empty for evermore.

But when Jack looked out of the window there was the Castle in the middle of the lake on its twelve golden pillars, and there was his young wife ever so pretty and gay in her nightcap looking out of the window too.

So they lived happily ever after.

ILLUSTRATIONS

— IN COLOR —

PAGE

JACK THE GIANT-KILLER

The giant Cormoran was the terror of all the country-side 21

Taking the keys of the castle, Jack unlocked all the doors 25

*The giant Galligantua and the wicked old magician transform the
duke's daughter into a white hind* 32

MR. AND MRS. VINEGAR

Mr. and Mrs. Vinegar at home 53

And that is the story of Mr. and Mrs. Vinegar 57

TATTERCOATS

Tattercoats dancing while the gooseherd pipes 64

DICK WHITTINGTON AND HIS CAT

Many's the beating he had from the broomstick or the ladle 85

When Puss saw the rats and mice she didn't wait to be told 89

ILLUSTRATIONS

PAGE

CATSKIN

She went along, and went along, and went along 99

THE STORY OF THE THREE BEARS

"Somebody has been at my porridge, and has eaten it all up!" 107

JACK AND THE BEANSTALK

"Fee-fi-fo-fum, I smell the blood of an Englishman." 129

THE FISH AND THE RING

The fisherman and his wife had no children, and they were just longing for a baby. 141

THE BOGEY-BEAST

"Well!" she chuckled, "I am in luck!" 149

THE TWO SISTERS

"Tree of mine! O Tree of mine!
Have you seen my naughty little maid?" 157